S0-ABB-692

Green Ivy Publishing
Lincoln Centre
8W140 Butterfield Road
Suite 1500
Oakbrook Terrace IL 60181-4843
www.greenivybooks.com

ISBN: 978-1-943955-00-8

REFLECTIONS FOR DAILY LIVING

(VOLUME ONE)

A Collection of Scriptural Reflections of
Rev. Jude Thaddeus Osunkwo

Contents

Introduction

God speaks to us through the words of the Sacred Scripture an· through the words of the Sermon.

We read from the Sacred Scripture concerning Jesus: "And beginnin· with Moses and all the Prophets, he explained to them what was said i· all the Scriptures concerning himself.... They asked each other, "Wer· not our hearts burning within us while he talked with us on the roa· and opened the Scriptures to us?" (Luke 24: 27.32). Recounting the Post Resurrection Emmaus encounter with Jesus and two of his disciple· (Cleopas and the other) within the context of "preaching and meal· Luke brings to the fore the all-time truth that "The Pulpit" and "Th· Table" (the table which Jesus left in the "Upper Room") are still presen· in His Church and will continue to be present until Christ comes agai·· It also underscores the interpenetration of the Word and the Eucharist·

On this interpenetration, Vatican Council 11 dogmatic Constitutio· on Divine Revelation *Dei Verbum* n. 21 states: "The Church has alway· venerated the divine Scriptures just as she venerates the body of the Lor· since, especially in the sacred liturgy, she unceasingly receives and offer· to the faithful the bread of life from the table both of God's word and c· Christ's body..."For the word of God is living and active" (Heb. 4:12) an· "it has power to build you up and give you your heritage among all thos· who are sanctified" (Acts 20:32; see 1 Thess. 2:13)".

Borrowing the words of the Unites States Conference of Catholi· Bishops, today "more than ever…an increasingly important objective c· the Sunday homily in our day is to stir the hearts of our people, to deepe· their knowledge of the faith, and to renew their living the faith in th· world and participation in the Church and her Sacraments". (USCCI· PREACHING THE MYSTERY OF FAITH, *http://www.usccb.org/belief· and-teachings/vocations/priesthood/priestly-life-and-ministry/uploa· usccb-preaching-document.pdf.*) This is why, in announcing 2012-13 ·· a "Year of Faith", Pope Benedict XVI declares: "What the world is i· particular need of today is the credible witness of people enlightened i· mind and heart by the word of the Lord, and capable of opening the hear· and minds of many to the desire for God and for true life, life without en·

Pope Benedict XVI, *PortaFidei(www.vatican.va/holy_father/benedict_vi/motu_proprio/documents/hf_ben-xvi_motu-proprio_20111011_orta-fidei_en.html)*, no. 15) Giving further instruction on the Homily, Pope Benedict in *Sacramentum Caritatis*, no. 46 called on preachers to rudently, with respect and thoughtful use of language, offer the faithful thematic homilies covering the great themes of the Christian faith" Pope Benedict XVI, Post-Synodal Apostolic Exhortation, *Sacramentum aritatis n.46).* Pope Francis cautions: "Whoever wants to preach must be he first to let the word of God move him deeply and become incarnate 1 his daily life". In this way, preaching will consist in that activity, so ntense and fruitful, which is "communicating to others what one has ontemplated", as St. Thomas wrote. God wants to make use of preachers is living, free and creative beings who let his word enter their own hearts efore passing it on to others. Christ's message must truly penetrate and ossess the preacher, not just intellectually but in his entire being". (Pope rancis, Apostolic Exhortation, *Evangelii Gaudium*, n.150) *http://www. atican.va/holy_father/francesco/apost_exhortations/documents/papa-ancesco_esortazione-ap_20131124_evangelii-gaudium_en.html.* Pope rancis adds: "A preacher has to contemplate the word, but he also has) contemplate his people.... He needs to be able to link the message of a iblical text to a human situation, to an experience that cries out for the ght of God's word. This interest has nothing to do with shrewdness or alculation; it is profoundly religious and pastoral.... There is no need) talk about the latest news in order to awaken people's interest; we ave television programs for that....It is possible, however, to start with ome fact or story so that God's word can forcefully resound in its call to onversion, worship, commitment to fraternity and service, and so forth". Pope Francis, Apostolic Exhortation, *Evangelii Gaudium,*n.154) *http:// 'ww.vatican.va/holy_father/francesco/apost_exhortations/documents/ apa-francesco_esortazione-ap_20131124_evangelii-gaudium_en.html*

In this book, *Reflections for Daily Living*, Rev. Dr. Jude Thaddeus kenna Osunkwo has applied and juxtaposed the four major traditional enses of interpreting the Sacred Scripture that are available to Preachers: ie Literal or Historical Sense (intended meaning by biblical author); ie Allegorical Sense (reading into biblical events and symbols, e.g. the

Red Sea and baptism); the Moral Sense (how scripture guides us to ac justly); the Anagogical Sense (relating biblical events and symbols t eternal destiny).

This Volume of *Reflections for Daily Living* is predominantly collection of original reflections of Fr. Osunkwo, from the Liturgica Scripture readings of Sundays and Weekdays as contained in th Roman Missal, done within the context of Eucharistic celebration. I it Fr. Osunkwo has tried, therefore, to satisfy that ultimate goal of good sermon which should be **to lead** people into a loving and intimat relationship with the Lord Jesus Christ (a relationship that forms th character of their persons), **to help** people to see sermon's connection with daily life, and **to guide** people in living out their faith. The aim is t illumine the human mind, touch the human heart and influence huma actions positively. In any good sermon, the "word" has to "take flesh" c it remains a mere ideology. *Reflections for Daily Living* is written in th present tense even when referring to past events. This is deliberate t recreate the context in the "Now" for the reader.

For profound understanding and maximized profit, it recommended that users of *Reflections for Daily Living* should prayerfull and meditatively go through the Scripture reading(s) preceding eac homily first before digesting it.

Exodus 20:22-24

Our Spiritual Foundation

Friend, the Creation account in the book of Genesis chapters One and two remind us of our beginnings. However, creation and redemption are tied together: salvation history is all about God's invitation to each and to all to share in his Divine life and love made perfect in Christ Jesus. This offers us opportunity to reflect on how we have responded and can still respond to this Divine invitation.

Our spiritual foundation is built around three "Altars". The three come together to form a strong spiritual foundation for each Christian:

- The Sanctuary of the person
- The Sanctuary of the home (the cult of the family)
- The Sanctuary of the Church

A Sanctuary is a place where the divine dwells, and where worship and offerings are made to the divine, and where the divine blesses people.

In the text of Exodus 20:24, God says: "In whatever altar I choose for the remembrance of my name, I will come to you there and bless you".

God has chosen the sanctuary of our Hearts, the sanctuary of our Homes, and the sanctuary of our Church, and God ought to be real, active, present and effective in these Holy Places that he has erected for himself.

In Psalms 63:3 and 55:17, God reminds us that these are the sanctuaries where we see God's power and glory, and where we call upon God and he saves us.

- The Sanctuary of the Human Person (Cf. ICor. 3:16; 6:19- God is concerned with what we do with our personal lives: we must bear fruits worthy of repentance (Matt 3:8)

- The Sanctuary of the Home (family): This is the melting pot of all heavenly values. Christ Jesus comes into our homes as a special guest and blesses our homes (Cf. Psalm 128).

- The Sanctuary of the Church (Cf. Acts 2:42)- the major feature of this sanctuary is steadfastness: to the Word of God and

Teachings of the Church, to the Eucharist, to Prayers, and t faith-community Fellowship.

In Psalm 11:3, God says: "Foundations once destroyed, what can th just do?" It is important to understand that our enemy the devil is inter on destroying these altars upon which the spiritual foundation of ou lives has been laid. Therefore,

- Resist the devil from destroying the altar that is your person

- Resist the devil from destroying the altar that is your home

- Resist the devil from destroying the altar that is your Church

In Psalm 55:16, God decrees: "They will go down who have evil i their hearts and homes".

God is able! Let us pray for healing and rebuilding of our altars—th altar of the Person, the altar of the Home and the altar of the Church–so that whenever we encounter God in these divinely erected altar (sanctuaries), we experience God's power, we experience God's glory, w experience God's blessings, we indeed experience salvation!

And as we pray for the healing of our altars and for the rebuildin and sustenance of our spiritual foundations, may we tirelessly work, b his grace, to stop the devil from attacking and afflicting these altars wit different harmful spiritual bacteria and viruses. Amen!

Sirach 44:1, 8-15

Our Family "Biological" and "Faith" Tree

Friend, when we think of the Sacred Heart of Jesus Christ, we remember God's infinite love for Humanity. This love has accompanied us from the time of our ancestors to our own generation; and will indeed be with us until we abide in glory with that LOVE WHO IS ETERNAL.

Today, if we try to reflect on our various Family biological trees as well as our Family Faith trees (and I would recommend that you read the whole of the letter to the Hebrews, Chapter Eleven), we see many things for which we must continue to thank God; We also see a few issues for which we must ask for Divine intervention.

In all, God has remained faithful to our generations. And what we we God is to have faith in him, to believe in him and to trust him (Cf. Matt 9:27-31).

The Blessed Apostle Paul in his letter to his spiritual son, Timothy, acknowledged Timothy's family faith tree and admonished him thus: "I remember your genuine faith, a faith that dwelt first in your grandmother Lois, and your mother Eunice, and now I am sure dwells in you as well".

For our own generation to prosper, we need to work along with God in Christ Jesus, believing and trusting him the more, accepting in our lives that God is real, active in our lives and present to us, affirming that His promises are ever true and that God never deceives, and ultimately totally surrendering our past, present and future to him. We pray that we may remain thankful and faithful to God for our various family and faith roots. Amen!

3.   Isaiah 11:1-10

Co-Existing Despite our Differences

Friend, it is God's wish to make us better human beings and bette Christians. In the Gospel of our Lord Jesus Christ according to Luke 3:1 6, John the Baptist cries out to us to prepare a highway way for the lor to have a smooth ride into our hearts.

Dear friends, can we ask for God's grace to help us work on th negative sides of our lives, those traits in us and some animal-lik instincts that do not conform to gospel principles, so that we can live i peace and harmony with one another and with God, in our homes, i our neighborhoods, in our Church, and in society.

In Isaiah 11:1-10, God announces the Messianic kingdom wher there will be such an overflowing peace that naturally incompatibl animals would live together in harmony. Any normal human perso would at least dream to enjoy such an environment.

But this Bible periscope and the picture of the animals it paints ref indeed to human beings.

Some of us at times act like wolves: we grab and cheat. Often, we ar not honest and faithful partners in our contracts and dealings with oth people – *"oburu ogbalaga; ihe onye ozo baa gi aka, o gala nkporo mkpur oka!"*.

Some of us at times act like lions: when we roar, every other perso takes cover – *"obere ihe metu, O chowa iji ukwu agbawa uzo!"*.

Some of us at times act like dogs: we are quite playful but unpredictabl – we can suddenly become dangerous when least expected.

Some of us at times act like snakes: we are crooked, nev straightforward with people, and operate with a dangerous philosoph of life which holds that *"agwo ga-elo ibe ya, O gaghi ebu!"*.

Some of us at times act like bats (*Usu*): we appear good in the day bu do bad things under the cover of darkness – *"ndi oji abali aga!"*.

Some of us at times act like adders (*Ebiogwu*): we sting whomeve comes around. We have "stings" in our mouths – *"Onu ha rere ere; On ha bu nsi!"*.

Some of us at times act like chameleons: we have no strength of character. What we do is determined by where we find ourselves at any particular time, be it among Christians or pagans, pioneers or drunkards, good or bad people – never stable!

Yet, some can manifest all of these traits: we may behave like wolves, and at other times lions; even at other times snakes, and adders, and rats, and chameleons.

However, like the innocent lamb and the little child, we can become innocent and sincere in dealing with one another, without having skeletons in our cupboards. Our human relationships can become more humane and genuine when we stop deceiving one another.

We can overcome our irreconcilable tendencies in our Christian living only by God's grace. And this is our challenge in today's society: to rediscover honesty and sincerity as we relate with people. We ask for the Eucharistic grace to begin to live in a more honest and sincere manner despite our individual differences because with the power that comes from God's Word, even natural incompatibles can enjoy supernatural harmony. May God be praised. Amen!

4.   Mark 8:27-35; James 2:17

Discipleship and the Cross

Friend, each Friday following the 24th Sunday in the Church liturgical year, we celebrate the feast of the exaltation of the Cross. Ever year at this feast (September 14), God reminds us that there is salvatio in the cross; there is victory in the cross.

In this gospel test, Jesus insists that each of his followers and discipl carry the cross. Jesus never loved carrying the Cross, as you kno HOWEVER, HE ACCEPTED CARRYING IT FOR THE GOOD O ALL OF US. There is a difference between loving to carry the Cross an accepting to carry the Cross.

In an era when most people would not carry any cross in life or bea any burden for others, Jesus insists: "Whoever wishes to come after n must deny himself, take up his Cross daily and follow me".

Dear friends, our crosses are hidden beneath the burdens of ou family life, which we have to carry daily; our crosses are hidden beneat the burdens of Church life, which we have to bear for Christ; and ou crosses are also hidden beneath the burdens of socio-cultural, socic political and socio-economic obligations, which we have to fulfil for th common good.

Our true discipleship includes carrying these challenging obligatior (crosses and burdens) of life in a way that promotes gospel values, neve compromising our Faith at any point, and never preferring comfort t goodness, nor falsehood to truth.

Jesus assures us in this gospel passage that when these crosses ai carried with resilience and with our eyes constantly turned on thin; that last forever; then, our efforts and labors will bear everlasting fruit Christ invites us to be ready to carry the burdens that faith and life mu place on our shoulders, and of course by his grace.

And God reminds us through Blessed Apostle James that faitl becomes salvific when expressed through good works.

We pray that Christ, who has asked us to carry our crosses and follo him, will continue to give each child of God his divine refreshment i our souls, his divine peace in our hearts and homes, and his divir isitation in our needs without which we cannot carry the burdens that life and faith place on our shoulders. His grace will never allow us to give up or give in, for if God leads us to it, he will surely lead us through it. His grace will ensure that none of our problems will see the end of us, but we will see the end of all our problems. Amen!

5.   Mark 9:30-37; James 3:16-4:3

The "Big Guns" and the "Small Guys" Mentality

Friend, in the gospel text above, "the disciples had been arguin on the way who was the greatest among them....Jesus took a child an placed it in their midst".

It is again the battle of the "big guns" versus the "small guys" (playin big and playing small). In the Bible, God has most often seemed to k on the side of the small guys. Come to think about it: Cain and Ab (Genesis 4); Ishmael and Isaac (Genesis 21); Esau and Jacob (Genes 25:19-26); his elder brothers and Joseph (Genesis 37); his elder brothe and David (1Samuel 16:1-13); Leah and Rachel (Genesis 29:15-30 Adonijah and Solomon (1Kings 1); Elder son and Prodigal son (Lul 15:11-32); Martha and Mary (Luke 10:38-41).

However, we must understand the message Christ is driving home t us in this gospel incident: the "big guns/small guys" here is more abot mentality and attitude than about age or physical size.

The Big Guns' mentality, as displayed in the argument by the discipl on the way, is one dominated by rivalry, competition and confrontatio On the other hand, the Small Guys' mentality is dominated k cooperation, collaboration and team spirit.

In the Biblical text of James cited above, God laments the level o tension and degree of devastation that the "big guns" mentality ca inject into human relationships. It is this mentality, founded on earth wisdom that often generates jealousy, selfish ambition, disorder, fov practices, conflict, envy and the "sizing-ups", which we notice often i our human relationships, and which God condemns through Blesse Apostle James.

On the other hand, the "small guys" or "children-like" mentality o co-operation, collaboration and team spirit founded on heavenly wisdor generates cleanness of heart, peace, gentleness (goodness), complianc mercy, good fruits (Cf. Matt 5; Galatians 5).

God appreciates the "small guys" mentality and he is always on th side of all who are humble. Jesus Christ recommends this mentality fc his followers. *"I bugowe onwe gi n'elu oji, oju gi isi. I butuo onwe gi ala, i juo gi oyi*" (If your arrogance places you on top of the iroko tree, you become crazy. But if you become humble, you enjoy peace of mind).

The "little child" in the quoted gospel has nothing to do with whether we are nine or ninety-nine years old – it has to do with our mentalities, our attitudes towards life.

The critical challenge that Jesus Christ throws at us is that believing and following him becomes possible when we become young-at-heart, i.e., when we predominantly co-operate with one another in an atmosphere of innocence and peace. The "big gun" mentality in our context, with its underlying attitude of rivalry, competition and confrontation, loses. The "small guy" mentality in our context, with its underlying attitude of co-operation, collaboration and team spirit, wins.

May God heal our heads (*ihe no anyi n'isi ka nku),* renew our hearts, and help us to improve our relationships. Amen!

6.   Luke 24:35-48; 1John 2:1-5a

Post Resurrection 1st Generation Christian Community and US

Friend, in this gospel text and other similar ones, we see the risen Jesus continually coming to his disciples to prove to them that he is alive and to define their mission. And they recognized him. Though not in the physical flesh, the risen Lord continues to come to us, and we recognize him through faith as one who lives in our midst. Jesus is present to us in the Eucharist. Jesus is present to us when we gather in his name. Jesus is present to us when we pray. Jesus is present to us through the word of the Scripture. Jesus is present to us through the Sacraments. Jesus is present to us during the many times we feel divine impulses in our hearts.

God, through Blessed Apostle John warns that if we think we know God, we must live as he commands or we become "living liars". In the book of the Acts of Apostles, mother Church has recorded for us and continues to present to us the first generation Christian community because we can learn a great deal from **how they lived and how they identified with the life and mission of the risen lord**, and how ourselves, Christians of today, can live together in peace and harmony with one another.

The first question is: How did they live? The implications of the answer for us today are not about 'the letters of their deed" but about "the spirit of their deeds". For example, many of them, like Barnabas, sold everything they owned and brought the proceeds to the apostles for the good of all (Cf. Acts 4:32-37). We are not quite able to do this today, but we can learn from their actions the spirit of sharing and fellow-feeling.

However, theirs was not a perfect society as it would appear. They had their struggles with imperfections and their problems to grapple with; we remember the rift between Jewish and Gentile Christians over the criteria for becoming a Christian which was solved by the first ecumenical council of the church in Jerusalem (Acts 15:1-35); we remember, too, the rift between Jewish and gentile Christians over tilted sharing of food to their widows (Acts 6:1-7); we also remember the misunderstanding between Peter and Paul during which Paul accused Peter of Hypocrisy

nd double standard (Galatians 2:11-14). The inspiring lesson in all this is
1at they were able to handle their problems, overcame their differences,
ut them behind and moved on.

Brothers and sisters, we are all "wounded healers" in Jesus Christ.
Ve must continue to improve on our individual and group spiritual
strengths" while submitting our "weaknesses" to the healing and
ansforming grace of God in Christ.

The other question is: How did they evangelize? The first generation
hristians carried out mission with Easter power because they were able
ɔ leap beyond the fear, timidity and despair of Good Friday to a life
f courage, boldness and confidence of Easter Sunday. Fear gave in to
ourage, timidity gave in to boldness, and despair gave in to confidence.

As Christians, we must continue to strive to become courageous
hristians, bold Christians, and confident Christians, no matter the
ircumstances. How else can we win the crown if there is no race? How
lse can we give the testimony if there is no test? And how else can we be
onquerors if we do not fight? May the Holy Spirit continue to enhance
ur spiritual boldness, enliven our spiritual confidence and strengthen
ur spiritual courage. Amen!

7.   Luke 3:1-6

Interior Renovation

Friend, Advent is a time of interior renovation, not only of our homes, but of our hearts. The forerunner of Jesus, John the Baptist, talk of preparing a highway for the Lord. This is not the highway that run from your city to another; it is the highway into our hearts that will mak it possible for Jesus to have an easy ride into our hearts at Christmas.

There was once the baptism of a little child in the church. Whe the Priest finished vesting, he asked the mother, "Are you ready?" Th Mother answered, "Yes father. I made some appetizers and cakes an cheese". And the father of the child added, "I've also some bottles of bee and a keg of whiskey, those will be enough".You may laugh. But is you preparation of Christmas any different from theirs? The season of adven is a time for Christians to prepare for the coming of the Lord. We thin of the three comings of the Lord: the three senses of Advent.

- Past: preparing to celebrate the human birth of the messiah, Jesu Christ

- Future: anticipating his second coming at the end of the world

- Present: embracing the situations and daily circumstances of ou lives (good and bad) as moments of grace though which the Lor continues to come into our lives daily as individual Christia and as the community of the people of God. Take your mind t your bank account. How much do you have in your account? Tak your mind to your assets. What are they? If you drop dead nov what happens to them? They will be gone from you, instantly. Bu something will be there for you; your spiritual deposit is in God bank. The question we need to be asking ourselves is this: Ho much have I been able to deposit into my spiritual bank all th while I have been a Christian through baptism?

In this gospel text, John the Baptist, quoting Isaiah, presents th images of mountains and valleys and crooked roads in our lives. Let u look at what they mean for us in our spiritual life as God has some wor always to do in us:

- Mountains: What are the sources of your arrogance that mak you look down on others?

- Valleys: What are the sources of your depression that make you have a poor image of yourself, and always think you are nobody?

- Rugged Roads: What are the habits that make you appear crooked, nasty, irritable, reckless and portray your relationship with others as insincere?

God, therefore, invites us to use this holy season of advent to improve in our spiritual fortunes so that we can continue to enjoy his peace, happiness, joy and glory.

May the Word of God continue to warm our hearts, and may the Eucharist continue to open our eyes to recognize and follow Jesus Christ. Amen!

8.   Mark 10:46-52; Hebrew 5:1-6
Bartimaeus: Who is Really blind? And Who Sees?

Friend, letter to the Hebrews Chapters 4:14-16 and 5:1-6, presen
Jesus as Priest. Once upon a time, a member of the group in Nigeria wh
call themselves Watchman Charismatics told me that it is not scriptur
for one to be addressed as a Priest. What is your opinion?

In the gospel of our Lord Jesus Christ according to Mark, Jesus dea
with the issue of blindness. The issue here goes beyond the Physic
blindness of Bartimaeus, which might affect the body, to the mo
problematic blindness of the mind, which can throw the human soul in
deforming blindness. We must always remember that whoever suffe
from what is described as "one-dimensional vision" (i.e. the aptitude
seeing things only from one myopic point of view) is relatively blin
This "failure to see reality" type of blindness is the most debilitating for
of blindness = the narrow way you see yourself and others, the narro
way you view things, the narrow way you handle issues.

Let us draw four points from this encounter between Bartimae
and Jesus:

- Bartimaeus knew and accepted the truth that he was blind
  admitting reality. Do you admit your limitations?

- Bartimaeus was resolute in moving against his limitations. Ho
  hard do you work to overcome your limitations? In the midst
  many voices and forces trying to stop him, he also recognize
  the voices and forces on his side – Do you only hear and see
  life the voices and forces fighting you? Why not also hear and se
  the many other voices and forces working for you. Do not be to
  pessimistic in life. Be always optimistic and positive. This is mo
  uplifting.

- Bartimaeus' admittance of his limitations and his courage
  move forward attracted the compassion, empathy (not sympath
  and kindness of God. Jesus responded to his leap of Faith. D
  you recognize the many times Jesus' voice invites you to come
  him?

- Bartimaeus' physically restored vision also brought in divine—spiritual—light into his entire life. He became an ardent follower of Jesus Christ. How has Jesus' miracle in your life made you a better Christian?

I want you to sing with me this inspirational song:

Amazing Grace! How sweet the sound!

That saved a wretch like me!

Am once was lost, but now am found!

Was blind, but now I see!

Amen!

9.   Matthew 23:1-12; 1 Thessalonians 2:7b-9

The Christian Example: Responsibility before Status

In one of the Faith communities where I served as a Pastor, we ha an election of new officers to assist me in the running of the communit Five months into their assignment, the Vice Chairperson wrote me th: message: "Good day, Fr. Jude. I am not really your assistant because is now a year since the election. When you put my name and the ne officials where we belong in the church bulletin, then I will know th you have accepted me to work with you. Be blessed in the name of Jesu Christ amen." This Vice Chairperson to me thought she had spent on year in office when actually she had spent just five months; and for he what matters most is having her name in the Parish bulletin and no the responsibility of her office.

Friend, in this gospel passage of Matthew, Jesus Christ rebukes th scribes and Pharisees of his time who sought to dominate rather tha to serve, who had to put status in society before responsibility to Go and humans, and who wanted to be treated differently from othe and indeed revered. Jesus, in so doing, uses the opportunity to cautio his followers to shun such divisive tendencies. Have we not only on master, the Christ, and one father, God? Are we not all brothers an sisters?

Jesus, our supreme master, is teaching us that no one shoul dominate the others, but everyone must be at the service of all, an especially those who have responsibility in the Christian communit must always be in the mood to serve.

This is a direct indictment of what could be described as "lu for honor titles and insatiable quest to be treated preferentially". A brothers and sisters, none should consider himself or herself superic to others. Our relationships in the family, in the church and in th society should not be a matter of superior and inferior but a matt of partners and collaborators in a good course. Thinking especial of our Igbo culture and Nigerian environment in which "elitism" ha preference to a life of simplicity (note that being simple is not the sam as being simplistic), we must be careful to avoid stepping on others imb up the political, economic or social ladder (*Agwo n'eloghi ibe ya naghi ebu!*).

Jesus invites us to take to the example of Blessed Apostle Paul, in he biblical text above, who gives us his own selfless service to Christ nd His Church as an example of responsible leadership.

May the Word fill our hearts with warmth for the love of God. And ay the Eucharist open the eyes of our hearts to recognize and follow 'hrist. Amen!

10.   Luke 2:1-14

The Prince of Peace is born for Us - Our Peace!

Friend, on this day, the Prince of Peace has been born for us. ↑ a world torn apart by divisions, wars, hatred, the Prince of Peace indeed born.

Before the birth of Jesus, Isaiah, the Old Testament prophet of "tl nativity of the Lord", gave him descriptive names: "Everlasting Fathe Wonderful counsellor, Mighty God, Prince of **Peace**" (Isaiah 9:5).

At his birth, the multitude of Angels descended from Heave singing: "Glory to God in the highest, and peace to men of good wil (Luke 2:13-14).

Appearing to his followers after his resurrection, Jesus said: "Pea be with you" (John 24:36).

At each Holy mass, Jesus continues to address each of his follower "Peace I leave you; my peace I give you" (Communion Rite).

Dear friends and fellow pilgrims on earth, to seek and cultiva peace is a fundamental aspect of our Christian faith and calling: Pea in our hearts, peace in our homes, peace in our Church communitie peace in our places of work and business, and peace in our world.

We have always talked much about peace, preached much abo peace. We must now sincerely move beyond "talking the peace tal to "living the peace". The ways I behave in the home, do they alwa promote peaceful co-existence? The ways I behave in the Church fami do they always ensure peaceful co-existence in the faith communit The ways I behave in my place of work or business or positions assignment, do they enhance peaceful co-existence?

As we celebrate Christmas, all of us are invited in the name of G to sincerely ponder our commitments to peace in our world: Ho much have we promoted practical peace? As we prepare to ask tl Lord to lead us into the New Year, each of us must make a resolutic in favor of peace: peace within me, peace with others, and peace wi God. Let us always pray, work and hope for a more peaceful life, a mo eaceful home, a more peaceful Christian community, a more peaceful arish and a more peaceful world. *A resolution for peace is indeed a esolution for God.*

May the Eternal Word and the Prince of Peace strengthen us; may His Body and Blood renew us. Amen!

11.   John 20:19-31; 1John 1:5-6

Celebrating Resurrection Victory as Empowered Witnesses

Friend, I love to sing this song every Easter of the lord's resurrection

Yes my Lord is able, he's able;

I know he's able, I know my Lord is able to see me through (DC)

For he has healed the broken hearted, he set the captive free;

He raised the dead; make the apostle work upon the sea...M lord...

Alleluia, the Lord is risen, let us rejoice and be glad! This is the responsorial and acclamation of today's celebration. At Easter, we celebrate the climax of the *triduum*. In the gospel reading from John, Jesus appears to the Apostles that very Easter evening to prove to them that Jesus is alive. The reason for our alleluia and rejoicing is that through the death and resurrection of Jesus Christ, we have been established upon sure part to salvation, and eternal life becomes a blessed assurance for all who accept him; that in Christ, our victory is assured, and we celebrate this victory (Cf. 1John 1:5-6).

And in the same Gospel, we are proclaimed, as were the apostle witnesses of the Lord's resurrection with a mission mandate; "Peace be with you! As the father has sent me, so I send you". In the Acts of the Apostles, we see the first generation Church already living out this witness and mandate.

Why are we qualified to be witnesses of the Lord's resurrection that happened in the past, we may ask? To answer this question, Cardinal Archbishop of Boston, Sean' P. O'Malley said in his 2012 Chrism Mass Homily: "Though we did not walk the streets of Palestine with Jesus as the Apostles did, we still receive the spirit that they received on Holy Thursday, Easter Sunday and Pentecost.... He did not need to remind the Apostles of their weaknesses, but went ahead to give the Spirit so that his followers will extend the love of God to all". In fact, the mystery of the death and resurrection of Jesus Christ is all about God's invitation to each and to all to share and to participate in his divine life and love made erfect and available in Christ Jesus.

This invitation to us to witness and to embark upon a mission must e heeded in the three sanctuaries of our lives: the sanctuary of our earts, the sanctuary of our homes and the sanctuary of the church.

What is a sanctuary? A sanctuary is a place where the divine dwells, nd where worship and offerings are made to him, and where the divine lesses men. In the book of Exodus 20:24b, God says: "In whatever anctuary I choose for the remembrance of my name, I will come to you here and bless you". By the death and resurrection of Jesus Christ, god as claimed the sanctuary of our hearts, the sanctuary of our homes and he sanctuary of the church, and he ought to be present and effective in hese Holy Places: in them we experience God's glory, power, blessings nd salvation. God is concerned with what happens to these his three anctuaries because "foundations once destroyed, what can the just do?" Psalms 11:3).

God expects that the sanctuary of the person (heart) must continue to ear fruits worthy of repentance (1Cor 3:16; 6:19; Matt 3:8). God expects hat the sanctuary of the home must continue to be the converging point f all Christian virtues (*Eziomume*). God expects that the sanctuary of he church to continue to be steadfast to the Word of God and teachings f the Church, to Eucharist, prayer and Christian fellowship.

By these, we become true witnesses of the Lord's resurrection and artakers in his mission. By God's grace, we must tirelessly work to stop he devil from attacking and infecting these sanctuaries with different piritual bacteria and viruses.

As we celebrate Easter Sunday, we affirm unequivocally that "God is ble and Jesus is Lord, and we pray that through our paschal experience, ;od will, by his grace, continue to strengthen and bless these sanctuaries ,ith the waters of baptism that wash us, the blood of Christ that nourishes s, and the spirit of truth that sanctifies us. Amen! And as we pray, the pirit pleads: Don't only keep the faith, spread it around.

12. Luke 4:10-18; Phil 4:4-7; Zephaniah 3:14-18a

Share! Care! Be Fair!

Friend, during each Advent season, God calls us through St. John the Baptist to make a highway for the lord. This is not a highway into our cities, but a highway into our hearts so that Jesus born at Christmas will have a smooth ride into our hearts with his "prosperity flowing like a river" (Isaiah 48:18). The Missalette calls Advent a time of "interior decoration": decoration not only of our homes, but more importantly of our hearts.

Today is *Gaudete* Sunday (Rejoice Sunday). Christmas is around the corner. Our rose candle is on and our candles in the Christmas wreath are burning.

The first reading from Prophet Zephaniah says: Rejoice, the Lord will renew you in love. The Responsorial from Isaiah 12:6 says: Cry out with joy and gladness. The second reading from St. Paul's letter to the Philippians says: Rejoice in the Lord always and have no anxiety; the peace of God will guard your hearts! Yes, because we are about to celebrate God's greatest gift to humankind: the gift of his son.

However, in the midst of these joyful invitations from God, to joy, to peace of mind and heart and to a life free of anxiety, we are often caught up in the web of bitter sorrow and unprecedented anxiety emanating from human actions or inactions.

Dear friends, especially at Eucharistic adoration, each time we ask the Eucharistic Jesus for divine refreshment in our souls, for divine peace in our hearts and in our homes, and for divine visitation in our life situations, these are not little words of prayer; these are weighty words of prayer. Pray these words every day. We should continue to remember that none of us is beyond the influence of the devil except by God's grace. Without God's refreshment in our souls, without his divine peace in our hearts and homes, the devil is capable of coming in and building his nest in human hearts – *ekwensu akuo akwu n'ime obi mmadu.*

We often talk and think of evil and Satan. Satan is a spirit. He operates in men and women we meet on our way every day who have given in o his wicked manipulations. We must, therefore, continue to thank God for protecting us from evil and from the evil one who manipulates people to cause others great pain.

Rather than destroy ourselves with violence, St. John the Baptist invites us in today's gospel to embrace in our lives the three words he addressed to the three groups respectively who approached him:

To the Crowd: Share!

To the Tax Collectors: Care!

To the Soldiers: Be Fair!

Share with one another. Care for one another. Be fair to all: three categorical invitations that ought to drive the engine of our human relationships and not bitterness, violence and murder. As we prepare to celebrate Christmas, and as we hand out gifts to friends and folks, let each person take home to his or her heart this timely advice of St. John the Baptist: No more bitterness, no more violence, no more murder. Rather, share, care, and be fair. Amen!

13.   Daniel 12:1-3; Psalm 23; Rev. 14:13;

Luke 12:35-40; Luke 23:33, 39-43

HE DIED? HE LIVES! (A Funeral Sermon)

Chetanu mbosi onwu nke g'adiri mmadu,

Anyi di ndu n'ututu, nwuru anwu n'anyasi,

Dika ahihia n'ime ofia, ndu anyi di nwankenke.

Jesu mere anyi ebere, Maria nyere anyi aka,

Jesu mere anyi ebere, Maria nyere anyi aka.

Friends, we have gathered here (in this Church) not just because ⟨of⟩ death, but above all because of life, especially life that is eternal. For ⟨a⟩ child of God, death opens the door to another life, and indeed the be⟨st⟩ life – the life of Blessedness in heaven with God. This is our Christia⟨n⟩ conviction, and that is why when one of our own passes on, we gath⟨er⟩ to fulfill an important obligation of our faith: to pray and conduct t⟨he⟩ rite of passage for loved ones who have gone before us marked with t⟨he⟩ sign of Faith, and to show solidarity and give support to the bereave⟨d⟩ family. This is the emphatic message from the biblical texts of Daniel a⟨nd⟩ Revelation (read them slowly).

God has indeed clothed man and woman with everlasting dignity ⟨by⟩ making us his children in Christ through his death and resurrection. W⟨e⟩ ought to claim this dignity and respond by living accordingly.

Friend, if each one of us were to choose the style of death, I d⟨o⟩ not know which style each of us would choose. However, the Gosp⟨el⟩ according to Apostle Luke 12:35-40 reminds us that we do not schedu⟨le⟩ death (anaghi eyi onwu eyi). Our exit from this world is as much ⟨a⟩ mystery as our entrance in to it. And both our African and Christia⟨n⟩ Traditions have Rites of Passage into and out of this world. What ⟨is⟩ important to us is how we live our lives; what is known to God alone ⟨is⟩ when, how and where we die.

It is also important that we note the emphatic message from Proph⟨et⟩ Daniel 12:1-3 that one does not die, and that's it. No! That's not it. W⟨e⟩

must all be raised to give account of all that we did here, and then go to where our actions and inactions have merited for each: either to eternal life or to eternal damnation. It is a blessed assurance, however that all those who live and die at peace with God are assured of Heaven because their souls are not lost but in peace, their death is precious to God, they will rest from their labors, they will not be separated from God in life and in death, and that they will reach the fullness of their lives (Cf. Wisdom 3:1-9; Psalm 116:7-9, 15; Matt 11:25-30; Romans 8:31b-35, 37-39; Psalm 40:10).

It is, therefore, very important that we live as to leave very positive impressions, not only in the minds and hearts of those who know us and those we have impacted, but also in the mind of God.

There are three levels of life open to us as humans, and any of the three (as of choice) has eternal consequences:

The Physykoi or vegetative life – this is the life we share with other lower animals and plants. Thus, we might usually hear people say: enjoy, life has no duplicate (unbridled materialism) let us eat today for tomorrow we shall die (hedonism); today is important, tomorrow does not matter (K'anyi biwe ndu, ebichaa ndu, amara ihe a ga-eme achi). The danger here is that people dominated by this level might forget that pleasure is meant for man and not man for pleasure. Sadly, some people live and die without going beyond this stage.

The Psychikoi or life controlled by reason, People here think. Those dominated by this level of life often forget that we are not just persons of the head, as Reason becomes their god. That is why one hears people say: if it is not reasonable, it is not meaningful. There is a forgetfulness here that life is larger than logic, and that human reason has need to be illumined by divine light. Unfortunately, some people live and die without going beyond this level.

The Pneumatikoi, or Spirit-led life, is that level of living where people allow divine light to control their physical bodies and rational minds. People at this level accept that the human person has a destiny determined by God. Thus St. Paul says: "I now live, no, not I, but Jesus lives in me... (Galatians 20:20). People who have attained this level of existence live and die in the blessed peace of God in Christ.

The Questions for us are: Where are you friend? And which of the three levels is your destination as evident in your words and deed actions and inactions? Is God leading, directing, and controlling you life as we pray in Psalm 23 always.

The Gospel text from Luke 23 (about the two thieves at either side of Jesus at the crucifixion) makes it emphatic that people can lose heaven not necessarily because of their human frailties, but because of their ba will towards, and affront to God and his grace.

The uplifting truth about our Christian hope in the abiding love of God for those who love him is captured in this biblical text from th Epistle of Paul: "For none of us lives for himself, and none of us die for himself. For if we live, we live for the Lord, and if we die, we die fo the Lord. So then, whether we live or whether we die, we are the Lord For to this end, Christ died and lived again that he might be Lord bot of the dead and of the living" (Romans 14:7-9). Indeed, love never die May this love of God, first poured into our hearts by the Holy Spir at Baptism and confirmation and renewed each time at the Eucharist table, continue to follow us from this mortal life, right into the grav and up from the grave into everlasting life. Friend, always remember to supplicate and atone for the dead (Cf. 1John 5:17; Revelations 21:2 1Corinthians 3:15; 2 Machabees 12:46; Luke 12:47-48). Pray for th dead, for death does not and cannot break the bond that exists in th Body of Christ. And the Holy Mass has always been the principal mean of this supplication and atonement. In Jesus Christ our good shepher and in the Church, may we continue to have the faith to live and th courage to die. Amen!

4. Luke 2:41-52; Sirach 3:2-6, 12_14; Colossians 3:12-21

The Holy Family of Jesus, Mary and Joseph, and Us

Friend, today is Family Sunday, the feast of the Holy Family. We all now in Genesis 2 how God instituted it, in Mark 10 how Jesus ennobled t, and how God has given us a model of the Christian family: THE HOLY 'AMILY. Friends, we must make marital love and family life work for us.

"The gift of marital love and family life is one of the most beautiful hings we have received from God. We must, therefore, continue to reasure it, nurture it, and promote the blessings and beauty of marriage nd family. No marriage should be allowed to die."

(Family Love and Life Series by Fr. (Dr) Judethadd Osunkwo).

In FAMILY LIFE AND LOVE: there are THINGS YOU MUST ;IVE AND RECEIVE: Remember always that "it is tasking to build a iouse but much more tasking to make a home". While building a house i more about resources, making a home is more about attitudes. There re things we must be willing to give and receive in order to make a iappy home of life and love together.

1. MUTUAL RESPECT: Respect is something you give and receive... n this case, always be the first "to yield the right of way".

2. FIDELITY AND TRUST: Your first reaction to this may be, "It i a non-issue". But remember pressures will mount from unexpected ources to test your love!

3. OPENNESS: We must always live above our own "ego" to accept ur mistakes and make amends!

4. COMMUNICATION/DIALOGUE: Do not become an Island; lways act in reference to and regard for other family members.!

5. MATURITY: Happy family love and life requires from adults, nature and not infantile behavior; this maturity includes emotional being balanced and not explosive); psychological (acting well); ntellectual (thinking properly); social (relating well); and spiritual rooted in God).

6. SENSITIVITY / ANTICIPATION: Be available and sensitive to the needs of the other; anticipate people around you.

We have dealt with some of the things we must be willing to give and receive in order to make a happy home of life and love together. We now turn to some of the things we must avoid:

1. Pride: putting status before responsibility.

2. Communication Gap: Acting without reference to others.

3. Selfishness: taking Exclusive advantage.

4. Undue Materialism: What I have I keep, and what I see I take!

5. Spiritual indifference: Living without being rooted in God!

6. Externalizing family issues: Trusting outsiders more than family members!

7. Disrespect for either biological family: We revere the family institution.

8. Being too argumentative: Arguing to win than yield to superior opinion.

9. False sense of Equality: Respect the fact that we are same and also different.

10. Lying: This undermines one's respect & leaves a scar in the mind

11. Odious Comparisons: No two families are the same!

12. Not available for family: The family is reason for all your toil!

5.   Hebrew 11:1-2, 8-9; Luke 12:32-48

Do You Have Faith?

Friend, what is Faith? What does it mean when someone says: I ave faith in God? Or what does it mean when someone is described as aving faith in God?

Vatican Council 1 defines faith as "intellectual ascent to God's word". rom this understanding, we got the prayer, Act of Faith (Omume nke ◦kwukwe).

But from the letter to the Hebrew Chapter 11:1-2, 8-9 about God and .braham, we see clearly that Faith is not about words and statutes; Faith ◦ncerns the movement of relationship between persons: between your erson and the person of God.

That is why the Catholic Church, in the synod of Bishops of 1974, ◦visited the definition of Faith of Vatican Council I. This Synod ◦defined Faith as "entering into and nurturing a personal relationship f friendship with God in Jesus Christ".

So for us Christians, Faith is all about relationship with God in Jesus hrist. This movement of friendship involves personal commitment and ◦nversion (metanoia) from the old self to a new life (born again) (Cf. ◦alatians Chapter 5).

In the real sense of it, therefore, Faith or having faith is not as simple ◦ knowing the Ten Commandments and their explanation; Faith or aving faith is not as simple as knowing all the Codes of the Canon w of the Church; Faith or having faith is not as simple as knowing by- ◦art all the books and all the verses in the Bible; Faith or having faith ◦ not as simple as knowing all the liturgical seasons, solemnities, feasts, ◦emorials and optional memorials of the Church; Faith or having faith ◦ not as simple as knowing and having a mastery the history of the ◦hurch from the birth of Jesus to the end of time; Faith or having faith ◦ not as simple as observing the prayers of the Church every day; Faith ◦ not as simple as participation in all the feasts of the Church; Faith is ◦t as simple as knowing and chanting all the hymns in the hymnal; ◦ith or having faith is not as simple as belonging to one or the other of

the Lay Apostolate Societies in the Church. Though these may promo
Faith; though these are pointers to Faith; though these serve Faith; the
are not Faith.

For the Christian, Faith is about a person-to-person life journey wit
God in Jesus Christ as evidenced in the call of Abraham and in his li
sojourns with God. So in the Church when we pray as the Apostles
Jesus did, "Lord, increase our faith", "Lord, Give us faith", Lord, give n
faith", we are simply saying: "Help me (us) to undertake a life journey
personal friendship with you (Jesus Christ)"

In this life journey of personal friendship with Jesus Christ, Jesu
tells us in the gospel just as God also told Abraham, "Do not be afraic
He promises to give us grace and to feed us so that we can grow in th
friendship with him.

It is to fulfil this promise that he orders his Apostles and the
successors (Ministers of the Church) in the gospel to feed the floc
diligently. So the Church continues to feed and nourish us especial
through the Preaching of the Word of God, through her teaching
through the sacraments especially the Eucharist in order to assist an
support us to continue to grow in our relationship of friendship wit
Jesus Christ and ensure growth in faith.

As the Church continues to feed and nourish us her children, ma
you continue to grow in faith, i.e. in your personal friendship with Jesu
Christ until death, as Abraham (our father in faith) did, so that the tru
homeland we seek above will be ours. Amen!

6. Jeremiah 38:4-6, 8-10; Hebrew 12:1-4; Luke 12:49-53

The Virtue of Fortitude

Friend, the Church teaches us that there are four Cardinal Virtues that regulate our everyday socio-cultural, socio-economic and socio-political lives. Without them influencing our lives positively, we are finished. The Cardinal Virtues (or moral or ethical virtues) are Prudence, Justice, Fortitude and Temperance (Cf. CCC Nos 1805-1809).

Fortitude is, therefore, one of the cardinal virtues. It is also called forbearance, long-suffering, steadfastness, for the sake of God (Cf. Matthew 5).

The Prophet of God, Jeremiah, endured shame and humiliation for the sake of the glory of God's name; Jesus endured shame, humiliation and death to accomplish God's will to save us. Both instances dramatically demonstrate the virtue of fortitude and its place in Christian life.

Commenting on today's readings, which prominently center on Christian Fortitude, the Church has this to say in CCC. 1808:

"*Fortitude* is the moral virtue that ensures firmness in difficulties and constancy in the pursuit of the good. It strengthens the resolve to resist temptations and to overcome obstacles in the moral life. The virtue of fortitude enables one to conquer fear, even fear of death, and to face trials and persecutions. It disposes one even to renounce and sacrifice his life in defense of a just cause. "The Lord is my strength and my song." 'In the world you have tribulation; but be of good cheer, I have overcome the world."

What else could have generated this spiritual energy except the fire, which Christ came to kindle and which he wished were already blazing. This fire in not the type that scotches and burns up everything on its way; it is that fire of Divine love that Christ enkindles and blazes in our hearts, which moves us to the conviction that nothing in this world is worth compromising my salvation for; nothing in this world is worth putting my soul at risk for; nothing in this life is worth dying for except to die for God. This fire of divine love pushes us to live, work and die for Him, who we believe in, and to insist on what we know to be right, no matter the opposition on our way.

This fire of Divine love in our hearts as Christians fortifies us to ▌strong, to continue to trust God, to continue to push, not giving in, givin up, throwing in the towel or calling it quits even when our marriage, o' family life, our jobs, our studies, our relationships are on trial (Cf. 1Pet 1:5-12).

God's top priority is to make us holy. In realizing this, trials can ▌a great benefit to our growth in the Lord, or it can become a destructi' barrier to our relationship with God. Trials produce maturity ar discipline (James 1:2-4). Trials help to cultivate compassion for othe (1Cor 1:3-4). Trials teach one to trust God's power alone (2Cor 1:1 4:7). Trials are the path to personal blessings and glory (Heb 2:9). Hum responses to trials are flight and fight. But supernatural responses trials are to rejoice (Col 1:24; 2Cor 7:4; James 1), to give praise (Job 2:1(to be strong-hearted (2Cor 4:1, 16; Heb 12:13), pray (James 5) and resist the devil (James 4:7).

Friends, any idea of Christianity without pain is an illusion, mirage. In this special year of faith, we pray for an increase of the virt of fortitude, forbearance, steadfastness, long suffering on Christians ar for the renewal in body, soul and spirit.

7.   Ecclesiastes 1:2, 2:21-23; Col 3:1-5, 9-10;

Luke 12:13-21

Human Greed

Friend, Jesus addresses us in the Gospel of John 15:15-16: "I no longer call you servants, because a servant does not know his master's business. Instead, I have called you friends, for everything that I learned from my Father I have made known to you. You did not choose me, but I chose you and appointed you so that you might go and bear fruit—fruit that will last—and so that whatever you ask in my name, the Father will give you"

The readings today center prominently on greed, that is, an untamed desire or passion to acquire and accumulate increasingly more possessions, even to the detriment of one's soul/salvation and one's relationship with God.

We must note that Jesus did not rebuff the petitioner in today's gospel (the young man) based on his seemingly simple request for settlement; after all, what is wrong in asking another, a third party, to adjudicate? Jesus, rather, rebuffed the young man based on an underlying greed hidden away in his heart.

Jesus, then, teaches in the ensuing parable of the short-sighted rich man that unwholesome accumulation of material things does not assure one's life and happiness.

Thus, Qoheleth reminds us in Ecclesiastes that all earthly possessions will pass, and only "who you are" will move on with you and not "what you have" (Cf. Job 1:12).

Jesus teaches that greed poisons the heart, eats away the soul and destroys relationships.

We, especially in Nigeria and Africa, know how much bickering, quarrels, bitterness and enmity issues of inheritance can often generate even in the closest of families because of greed. That is why the advice of Apostle Paul in Colossians is *ad rem* and appropriate: "Since, then, you have been raised with Christ, set your hearts on things above, where

Christ is seated at the right hand of God. Set your minds on thing above, not on earthly things. For you died, and your life is now hidde with Christ in God. When Christ—who is your life—appears, then yo also will appear with him in glory....Put to death, therefore, whatev belongs to your earthly nature: sexual immorality, impurity, lust, ev desires and greed, which is idolatry.... Do not lie to each other, since yo have taken off your old self with its practices, and have put on the ne self, which is being renewed in knowledge in the image of its Creator".

Commenting on the readings of today, the Church in CCC 172 says: "The beatitude we are promised confronts us with decisive mor choices. It invites us to purify our hearts of bad instincts and to see the love of God above all else. It teaches us that true happiness is n found in riches or well-being, in human fame or power, or in any huma achievement—however beneficial it may be—or indeed in any creatur but in God alone, the source of every good and of all love...."

What is God saying to us? – Take things easy my friend! Naked w came, naked we will go! (Jirinu ya nwayoo! Onweghi nke ebu ala mmuo

The bottom line: Do not put your lovely soul at risk just because material possessions!

8. Gen. 45:1-5,13-15 to 46:1-7,28-30; Gal 5:1,13-14;

Lk 10:1-9

Reconciliation and Healing

Friend, the book of Ecclesiastes 3:3 talks of "a time to heal". In the book of Galatians 5:1, 3-4, God calls out to us: As those who have been called in Christ, be led by the Spirit of freedom and no longer by the yoke of slavery; the Spirit of freedom helps us to serve one another in love; the yoke of slavery pushes us to bite and devour one another, and this consumes us. Here, God calls out to us as Christian brothers and sisters reject totally the yoke of slavery and embrace the Spirit of freedom that is found in Christ.

In our biological families, in our faith families, in our neighborhood families, in our job or business families, in our school families, we want to pray and work toward stopping the biting of one another, the devouring of one another, the bitterness against one another, the defaming of one another's name/character that dent our human horizon today. All of these yokes of slavery exist because people have pain in their hearts. We must continue to pray, therefore, for healing of hearts which only God can do to free our environment and relationships from this yoke that consumes us like wildfire.

The passage of the book of Genesis cited above deals with the reunification and Reconciliation that took place in Jacob's family, a biblical incident that can move any heart. We all know the bigger story: How mischief (aruruala) set in into the blessed family of Jacob through some of his children; that was the plot (nkata akpara) against Joseph: The Family was no longer the same again. The harmony had been broken and none was spared. They all lived with the pain (ufu na obi mgbawa). Often, cordial relationships give way to scheming and manipulation that often arise in human relationships due to false alarm or sense of nonexistent insecurity. Thus, in human relationships, persons can become actors in the scene of life, schemers and manipulators rather than genuine friends. This is the state of many relationships today in our world. **Jacob (Israel)** lived with the pain and difficulty of coming to terms with the story that his beloved son, Joseph, was dead "My son dead! And I did not see his corpse?"

Reuben, Judah and Benjamin: (unhappy with the plot again Joseph) lived with the pain of bitter resentment against the other eig brothers for their mischief, and the added pain of concealing the tru story of the plot to their father.

8 Brothers (Simeon, Levi, Issachar, Zebulun, Dan, Naphtali, Ga and Asher): Lived with the pain of discomfort and guilt of mischievo spirits.

Joseph: Lived with the pain of missing his family; despite his exalte position in Egypt, he was still miserable.

This was the situation in Jacob's family for so many years and no was spared. They must have all longed in their heart for an opportuni to reunite. But none could express it.

In the Genesis incident above, God provided them the opportuni for reunion and reconciliation. We read about their reunification: holdi themselves close to one another, close to their hearts, aged father and children, weeping, tears of pain and joy.

Imagine this scene in your mind. Imagine the feeling right in the bones of the peace of God once more invading their hearts.

Imagine their old father, Jacob, even making the super sacrifice accepting being uprooted from his natural base and taken to Egy only to ensure that his family was reconciled and reunited while he w alive. He says to Joseph and his brothers, "I can now die in peace" (Ka nwuzie, ozugoro M).

Imagine the words of healing that came from Joseph to his brothe (45:4-5): "Come closer to me. I am your brother, Joseph, whom you on sold into Egypt. But do not be distressed and do not reproach yourselv for having sold me...."

Imagine in your mind and heart the peace, the tranquility of hea and mind, the joy, the completeness, the blessing each of the 12 and the father must have experienced via this reunion.

We often live in denial. But the truth is that often there is cold w around (enwere nnukwu iron a obi ojoo n'agbata n'agbata, n'etiti anyi). T type of reunion that happened in the family of Jacob is what God wish to happen among us at all necessary levels. The fire of Divine love in o

earts always draws a battle line between Good and Evil in the world; and
e Christians are caught up in this battle line. We pray for God's grace.

Let each child of God reflect deeply on this incident and your condition
ith others. Do not allow this divine opportunity to heal slip by. No more
iding; no more burden bearing. It is time to trust God and to lay the
urden of unforgiveness and pain down for good; it is time to say "enough
enough" to any bitter feelings against one another; it is time to heal; it is
me to get up and move on.

In Psalm 80, God reminds us that we are part of the vine that his right
and has planted. And Psalm 42:5b-6a says:

"When I went in procession with the Crowd

I went with them to the house of God

Amid loud cries of thanksgiving

With the multitude keeping festival

Why are you downcast my soul?

Why do you groan within me?

When people come to Church to worship with brothers and sisters,
ney want to go home happy, joyful and in good spirit and not to go sad,
owncast or depressed. We all must ensure this to one another in charity.
e owe this to one another.

In God's name, I appeal to whoever feels hurt for whatever reason,
dministrative or personal, to accept God's grace and heal.

In this divine movement of healing, reconciliation and reunion, do not
bstruct God! Do not obstruct God! Do not obstruct God! (Anochkwarala
hukwu Uzo).

19 . Matt 2:1-12; Eph 3:2-3a, 5-6; Is 60:1-6

Epiphany: Our Manifestation

Friend, the three wise men from the East came with gifts: gold frankincense and myrrh.

One tradition has it that they were actually four with four gift the fourth among them being Attaban with the gift of precious ston signifying that the author of all goods has been born in a manger.

The Epiphany signifies that salvation is indeed available to all wh seek God with sincere hearts: the shepherds representing Israel and th three wise men standing for the gentiles: God continues to direct the on the road unto salvation.

But Herod and his cohorts represent the deceitful (ndi aghugho) an the mischievous (ndi uru): they shall always be God's enemies and sha always remain in the dark.

Today, we have no gold, or frankincense, or myrrh, or precious stor to give the infant born in the manger. But we have something mor precious to give: lives completely dedicated to him as God strives to b born into our hearts, into our homes and into our communities eac day.

May the heavenly star that announced the incarnation continue illumine our hearts, direct our thoughts and influence our actions. An may the peace of God continue to be upon all persons of good will.

0. Genesis 2:7-9, 3:1-7; Romans 5:12-19; Matthew 4:1-11

The Christian and Temptation

Friend, Ash Wednesday launches us into the holy season of Lent, the 0 days and 40 nights during which we more intensely seek reconciliation nd reunion with God as we prepare for the Easter celebration of our iumph in Christ as captured in the letter to the Romans.

On Ash Wednesday, God gave us the roadmap to our Lenten iscipline, and our faith demands it: Intensify your prayer (especially ersonal prayer), fast as much as your health can allow you. Give arms to ne poor borne of a pure intention to glorify God (Cf. Matthew 6:1-18).

The aim of the Lenten exercise should be the interior transformation f our hearts and minds, which should lead to a better relationship with iod and with our neighbors.

If our prayers, fasting, almsgiving, self-denial, abstinence, penance, o not lead to this interior transformation, they are useless (Cf. Is 58:1-).

In this text of Genesis, God tells man and woman that there is a limit what they have to do; they cannot do everything that they want. But atan tells man and woman: Do not mind God, you can do everything ou want. We all know the result of the devil's advice.

The devil returns: The gospel of today presents the temptations of sus by the devil.

In life, temptations will surely, and do surely come to each one of us.

Jesus was tempted with food probably because Satan knew Jesus was ungry.

Jesus was tempted with wealth probably because Satan knew Jesus as from a poor family.

Jesus was tempted with power probably because Satan knew Jesus ad been given all authority in heaven, on earth and in the netherworld y the Father.

In the face of temptation of food and pleasure, Jesus responded with self-control (agaghi m eri adachi uzo).

In the face of temptation of wealth, Jesus responded with contentme (oke m nwere juru m afo).

And in the face of temptation of power, Jesus responded wit moderation (nke m ji ka; riwe ya enyela m).

These virtues – self-control, contentment and moderation – star as a strong judgment against many of our choices, our appetite fo consumerism, our solicitation of profit and our unbridled ambition.

On the temptation of Jesus, Pope Francis has this admonition give: "Jesus decisively rejects all of these temptations and reaffirn his unwavering will to follow the path set by the Father, without an compromise with sin or the world's logic. Note well how Jesus replie He does not dialogue with Satan as Eve did in the earthly paradise. Jesu knows well that you cannot dialogue with Satan. Satan is quite astut For this reason Jesus, instead of talking to Satan as Eve did, chooses take refuge in the Word of God and answers with the force of this Wor Let us remember this: In the moment of temptation, in our temptation we should not argue with Satan, but always defend ourselves with th Word of God" (Quoted in *The Pilot*, 2014, Vol. 185, n. 11).

Today and through the period of Lent, ask yourself: From where an from what are my own temptations coming? And what are the virtu (ike eziomume) that I need in order to overcome temptations in my lif It is one thing to diagnose a need or problem and indeed admit that have this need or problem so as not to live in self-denial. But it is anoth issue to proffer, accept and seek the right solutions to the problem need.

When we have known the sources of our temptations, and the virtu we need to overcome them, then pray and ask Heaven for help. Chri prayed and fasted to be able to live the life, preach the Word and do th work of God. Let us use this period to fast and pray that the Holy Spi assists us in dealing with our temptations so as to live the life, preach th word and do the work of God.

And may the Eucharist, which we celebrate and receive, continue strengthen us in our resolve to be better Christians, better children God and better human beings. Amen!

1.   Sirach 3:17-20, 28-29; Luke 14:1, 7-14

Humility and Solidarity with the Poor.

Friend, some people see today's gospel as Jesus teaching table tiquette and **good manners** at a dinner. But in-between the lines, there much more than etiquette involved here. Jesus is teaching the basic hristian virtues of **humility** and **solidarity with the poor**. And he does is in today's gospel using two parables.

The first parable, on the One Invited to the Wedding Feast (verses -11) teaches of **the virtue of Humility (also echoed in the First eading).** It reminds us that as Christians who are invited to the feast f the Lord's Supper, irrespective of social status and importance, we me to the Eucharistic celebration (Holy Mass) as brothers and sisters equal standing before God. This is the only place where employer and nployee relationship, master and servant distinctions dissolve, and e recognize one another simply as brothers and sisters in the Lord, as gether we call God "Our Father.

The Letter of James condemns all un-Christian distinctions in the ouse of God this way:

> **If a person with gold rings and in fine clothes comes into your assembly, and if a poor person in dirty clothes also comes in, and if you take notice of the one wearing the fine clothes and say, "Have a seat here, please," while to the one who is poor you say, "Stand there," or, "Sit at my feet," have you not made distinctions among yourselves?** (James 2:2-4).

Jesus is challenging us, his followers, to eschew the rich-poor stinction mentality among us and to recognize and treat one another ith respect as brothers and sisters of equal standing before God. **"For 1 who exalt themselves will be humbled, and those who humble emselves will be exalted"** (Luke 14:11).

The second parable, on the One Giving a Great Dinner (verses 12-), teaches **solidarity with the poor.**

When you give a luncheon or a dinner, do not invite your friends r your brothers or your relatives or rich neighbors, in case they

may invite you in return, and you would be repaid. But when you give a banquet, invite the poor, the crippled, the lame and the blind (verses 12-13).

Jesus reminds us that as Christians, we should give priority to the poor and less fortunate (the poorest of the poor) in the way we administer and dispense our resources both as individuals and as Community Faith– this is part of our Christian obligations as it hinges on one of the cardinal pillars of our faith: Charity.

The challenging question is: Does our Faith Community measure up to the criterion of preferential option for the poor? Are we sure that our Faith Community activities and programs we **"invite the poor, the crippled, the lame and the blind"** (Luke 14:13). **How?**

2.   1 Timothy 1:12-17; Luke 15:1-32

Self-Examination & Acknowledgement of God's Mercy

Friend, in the reading from 1Timothy 1:12-17, we see Paul acknowledging his sins in a sincere self-examination that is at the same time open to God's mercy and forgiveness.

When we come together for worship, examination of conscience and acknowledgment of sin is part and parcel of our daily prayer and devotions.

Now, some Christians of the "I'm-okay-you're-okay" school of spirituality raise the objection that constant consciousness of one's sinfulness could lead to low self-image and self-hate, can make people spiritually immobilized and morose, no longer able to celebrate life.

This is unfortunate. Awareness of our sinfulness, when done in the right spirit, is a most healthy and empowering spiritual exercise. When Paul accuses himself to be the chief of sinners: "Christ Jesus came into the world to save sinners – of whom I am the foremost" (1 Timothy 15), it did not lead Paul to low self-esteem or depression. It led him to vibrant life of gratitude and praise to God and to humility toward God and neighbor in his ministry.

Awareness of our sins is just one side of the coin. Continually looking only at this one can depress anybody. But we should look also at the other side of the coin: this other side is God's mercy and forgiveness

In the Gospel (Luke 15: 1-32): In Jesus the son of God and through the compelling power of the Holy Spirit, we appreciate the compassionate love of God for us all as the Shepherd who searches out the one sheep that wandered off, the homeowner who turns the house upside down to recover a misplaced coin, the Father welcoming both sons to the celebration table and allowing each son to "come to his senses".

*Striking: Both sons needed repentance: One wandered into a mess; the other was at home but enmeshed in anger, bitterness, and resentment (Cf. CCC 1846-1848 on today's Readings):

Remember the popular saying of Jesus recorded twice in Luke: "All

who exalt themselves will be humbled, and those who humble themselv
will be exalted" (Luke 14:11; 18:14). Humility is indispensable in tru
Christian spirituality and nothing is more humbling than an awarene
of our sins, the various ways in which we have failed God, our neighb
and ourselves. Humility makes us more effective channels of God's lov

Maybe we can become better witnesses of God's love in our wor
today when see ourselves as forgiven sinners, inviting other sinners
come on and receive God's forgiveness as we have done, rather tha
presenting ourselves as holy people trying to save poor sinners from he

3.   Amos 8:4-7; 1Timothy 2:1-8; Luke 16:10-13

Mammonism (or Mammon Sickness)

Hymn: Riwe Ya Enyela M oh! (Onye Nna, Onye Nne, Youth, Fada, siter).

Friend, in this Gospel from St. Luke, Jesus makes a very categorical nd emphatic statement: "You cannot serve both God and Mammon" uke 16:13).

The word, "mammon" is an Anglicized Aramaic word. In Aramaic, ammon means money, property, possession.

Fr. John Haughey, SJ, in his book "The Holy Use of Money" identified ur symptoms of Mammonism or "mammon sickness":

- Desperate running after things

- Numbness in relationships

- Divided attention to God

- Trampling on the rights of others, especially the weak and the poor

You can use these symptoms to imagine and evaluate what happens business, in politics, indeed in our socio-economic activities and cio-political engagements.

This is precisely why, in this reading from Prophet Amos, God is buking people who indulge in dishonest business to rip people off r cheap gains, and warns that such actions attract God's anger – iji ghugho na akwuwaghi aka oto n'eme business n'akpasukwa Chukwu ve maka udi omume a bu mammonism (mammon sickness).

Again in the Reading from St. Paul's letter to St. Timothy, God dmonishes that we earnestly offer prayers and supplications for ll, especially for our leaders and all in authority, so that the spirit of ammonism does not overwhelm them and they turn around to oppress nd impoverish us: oburukwa n'anyi choro ka ume na obi ruo anyi ala, nyi kpewekwa ekpere maka ndi n'achi anyi ka mammon sickness ghara ibanye ha n'ime, ha ewee mee anyi aru, menyou anyi anya.

Listen to this from 1Timothy 6:6-12:

[6] "But godliness with contentment is great gain. [7] For we brough nothing into the world, and we can take nothing out of it. [8] But if we hav food and clothing, we will be content with that. [9] Those who want to g rich fall into temptation and into many foolish and harmful desires th plunge them into ruin and destruction, for the love of money is a roo of all kinds of evil[10]. Some people, eager for money, have wandered fro the faith and pierced themselves with many grief.

[11] But you, man of God, pursue righteousness, godliness, faith, lov endurance and gentleness.[12] Fight the good fight of the faith. Take ho of the eternal life to which you were called when you made your goo confession in the presence of many witnesses".

What is God telling us in all of this? The bottom-line is: Take thing easy! Do not compromise your soul because of material things! Pray fo God to give you enough to be comfortable and a little extra for chari and that is enough! K'anyi jirinu ya nwayoo! Onweghi nke ebu a mmuo!The CCC 2424 sums up mammonism this way: A theory th makes profit the exclusive norm and ultimate end of economic activi is morally unacceptable. The disordered desire for money cannot b produce perverse effects. It is one of the causes of the many conflic disturbing the social order. A system that "subordinates the basic righ of individuals and of groups to the collective organization of productio is contrary to human dignity. Every practice that reduces persons nothing more than a means of profit enslaves man, leads to idolizir money, and contributing to the spread of atheism. "You cannot ser God and mammon."

Friend, pray that God, by his grace, will give people the right attitud to material things so that people do not place material wealth or mone or possessions above their marriage, their family, their relationship their political and governmental responsibilities, their faith and the God. Amen!

4. Amos 6:1a,4-7; Luke 14:12-14; Luke 16:19-31

Solidarity with the Poor, No Complacency!

In the Gospel of St. Luke, Jesus states:

"When you give a luncheon or dinner, do not invite your friends, our brothers or sisters, your relatives, or your rich neighbors; in case they may invite you back and so you will be repaid. [13] But when you give a banquet, invite the poor, the crippled, the lame, the blind, [14] and you will be blessed. Although they cannot repay you, you will be repaid at the resurrection of the righteous."

Friend, this is a divine injunction especially to Christians, not only as individuals but also as communities of Faith, to show solidarity with the poor, the weak and the suffering.

In the readings of Amos 6 and Luke 16, the well-to-do in Amos and the rich man in Luke committed the sin of complacency: They were complacent to the needs of the poor and suffering around them (looking away when they could have used their position or their resources to make a difference.

Charity to the poor and suffering has its reward! Do not look away from anyone you can help! Do concrete charity. Let me challenge you: What is your plan to help somebody in need this week or this month or this year?

25.   Job 1:6-22

RESILIENCE IN TRIALS AND SUFFERING

Friend, the biblical figure of Job remains for us the symbol
Christian resilience in the face of suffering and utter dependence c
God. It reminds us of the reality of evil in the world and the suprema
of God over evil.

Verse 6: Notice here that God convoked a meeting for the childre
of God, and Satan also attended.

This tells us that Satan was still in denial that his condition was r
longer good with God and that he never belonged anymore; he is a fall
angel who still wants to belong.

Verse 8: Notice here God's posture before Satan, even as Go
questions the legality of Satan's presence. God interrogates Satan: Ha
you noticed my servant, Job...blameless, upright, God-fearing, ar
avoiding evil? Do you notice how God was boasting of his worthy chil

Do you see how good God feels when we are measuring up, doir
well and responding to his grace?

Verse 9: Notice the unhappy response of Satan who retorted to Go
You boast of Job, your servant because you have surrounded him and
that he has with your protection, blessings and grace.... Remove the
and he will profane and blaspheme against you.

Do you see how envious and jealous Satan can become at our Go
given blessings?

Verse 12: Notice God's reaction at Satan's unhappy complaint: Sata
you can go and try my servant, Job.... Remove anything that you wis
but do not lay a hand upon his person.

Who we are as persons is more important to God than what we hav
And who we are defines us before God and not what we have.

Verse 22: The Bible states here that in all his tribulations, Job did n
do anything disrespectful of God, nor did he utter a word against Hin

He remained constant, resolute, unyielding: utter resignation od's will.

Conclusion: Dear friend, Holy Child of God, no matter what you
re going through now, no matter what you feel that the devil is using
o afflict you and carry out an assault on you and yours, God will reign
upreme at the end of your faith-fight and you will surely overcome.

Sing with me:

We shall overcome

We shall overcome

We shall overcome somedayOh down in my heart, I do believe

We shall overcome someday

26. Habakkuk 1:2-3; 2:2-4; 2Tim 1:6-8, 13-14; Luke 17:5-1

FAITH THAT WORKS!

Friend, the dominating theme in these biblical texts is Faith.

In the text of Habakkuk God says: "The just one, because of h faith, shall live" (Hab 2:4). This means that faith brings life.

In the text from the Gospel according to Luke, Jesus affirms: "If yc have faith as little as a mustard seed, you can say to the mulberry tr 'move', and it will obey you" (Luke 17:6). This means that no matt how little your faith might seem, God can still perform wonders i you and through you. This loving invitation and challenge moved tl Apostles to pray in all humility and ask for an increase of faith.

In the text of Second letter of St. Paul to Timothy, Paul, eulogizir the faith that was in Timothy's Grandmother and Mother Lois ar Eunice respectively, admonishes Timothy to "fane into flame the gi (faith-mine) that you have received from God" (2Tim 1:6).

In this Special year of Faith, October 2012 through Novemb 2013 (as pronounced by Pope Emeritus Benedict XVI, the aim of o six *Year of Faith* talks has been to help us fan into flame the gift of fait that we have received from God.

Let us make a recapitulation of those Talks:

1. Faith in the Bible (Fr. Judethadd Osunkwo: Emphasis here w on the three levels of Faith:

*faith (okwukwe): Accepting that God is real, active and prese to me.

*belief (nkwenye): Credo, i.e., Giving my heart to His promis and to the eternal truth that God never deceives.

*total submission: "I am God's and God is mine" (ma k'oma, n k'ojo, n'aka gi Chukwu ka M hanyere onwe m).

2. The Creed (Fr. Romanus Onyekuru): Emphasized that this Faith must be lived, i.e., giving our lives totally to God the father, to Jesus Christ, to the Holy Spirit and to the Church. This also involves shunning the devil and all his deceitful attractions from idolatry, to divination, to fetishism (superstition), to occultism, etc.

3. Prayer (Fr. Ignatius Nwachukwu): Emphasized that this Faith must be expressed in prayer. Prayer is faith expressed; if you are not praying, your Faith dies.

4. Holy Mass/Eucharist (Fr. Christian Ohazurume): Emphasized that this Faith must be celebrated. Our faith is a celebrating faith and our Church is a celebrating Church. The climax of this celebration is the Holy Mass through which we receive the Eucharist: the Sacrament of Unity because when we receive Holy Communion, we become one with Jesus Christ and are united with one another. Always attend Holy Mass prepared!

5. Family Catechism (Sr. Christiana Onyewuche): Emphasized that this Faith must be made practical, i.e., practically shown in the manner we conduct ourselves and our children especially in the House of God, showing respect and reverence to God by the way we behave while in the Church.

6. Service as Mission (Mr. Raphael Ilona): Emphasized that this Faith must transform us into servants for one another in the bigger Church family: The Church is beneficial to you! How useful are you to your Church Community?

Friends, do you now see that a faith that works is faith that is **lived, xpressed, celebrated, made practical, transforming in which God real, active and present to you?** Dear friend, Faith is life. Even if ou have just a little of it, God is able to perform wonders in you nd through you. Fan your Faith, therefore, into flame. Move away 'om a dormant faith to a living faith. A living faith meets God in 1e Sacred Scripture; a living faith worships the Lord in the liturgy nd sacraments; a living faith serves the Lord in ministry; a living faith shines out in life commitment to God in the lay, or religious priestly states; a living faith responds to the social engagements th promote community; a living faith speaks and shares the good news

We pray that, putting the lessons from these talks into practic God will renew and transform us into better Christians as we prepa to bring this renewal into our activities and into our world.

7.

Hebrew 11:1-44

WHAT FAITH ENTAILS

Friend, the letter to the Hebrews 11:6 states categorically: "Without faith, it is impossible to please God".

What is Faith?

Hebrew 11:1 defines faith as "the acceptance of what is not seen and the expectation of what is hoped for" (Nnabata ihe di adi, ya na olile nya n'ihe di n'ihu).

Faith at Work

In the gospels, Jesus encourages a strong and unwavering faith and rewards it. This is clear in most of his Faith-based healings, exorcisms, nd people raised from death. He continues to say to them: "your faith as saved you" and not "I have saved or healed you".

- Look at the case of the Paralytic (Mk 2:5): "When Jesus saw their faith…".

- Look at the case of Bartimaeus the blind (Mk 10:52): "Go your way, your faith has saved you".

- Look at the case of the woman with the flow of blood for 12 years (Mk 5:34): "Daughter, your faith has saved you. Go in peace and be cured of your affliction".

- Look at the case of the ten lepers (Lk 17:19): "Stand up and go, your faith has saved you".

- Look at the case of the Canaanite woman's daughter possessed by a demon (Matt 15:28): After 3 shockers, Jesus says: "Oh woman, great is your faith. Let it be done to you as you wish".

- Look at the case of the epileptic mute boy (Mk 9:23): Before exorcising the epileptic spirit tormenting him, Jesus says to his father: "Everything is possible to one who has faith".

- Look at the case of the dead daughter of Jarius (Mk 5:36): Jesus says to his father, "Do not be afraid, just have faith".

Lack of Faith

There are some instances in the Gospel where Jesus rebukes h followers for lack of faith, and this rebuke would have become loud and stronger if Jesus were to be physically here with us today:

- Matt 8:26: Look at the incident of the storm: "Why are you afra oh you of little faith".

- Lk 8:25: "Where is your faith?".

- Matt 17:20: "Where your faith the size of a mustard seed….".

- Mk 16:14: The Resurrection story.

Reaction of Disciples

Lk 17:5: "Lord, increase our faith". This ought to be the sincere pray request of child of God every day.

What Faith Entails

Hebrew 11:1-44 mentions some of our ancestors in Faith: Ab Enoch, Noah, Abraham, Isaac, Jacob, Moses, Gideon, Barak, Sampso Jephthah, David, Samuel, Mother of 7 sons of Macchabees. In all th people mentioned, we can identify three levels of faith:

- faith (okwukwe): accepting that God is real, active and present us.

- belief (nkwenye): giving the heart to (credo) the truth of h promises and that God never deceives.

- total surrender (nhanye onwe): inner personal assurance that am God's and God is mine (ma k'oma, ma k'ojo, n'aka Chukwu m hanyere onwe m).

But Apostle James reminds us that faith goes with good wor (James 2:26). Thus, this **faith must witness, share, invite:** witness wi your good life, share your faith with others (don't just keep the faith yourself, spread it around) and invite people back to the Church. But we are not strong in our faith, we are incapable of any of these.

Friend, do you see now that Faith is not so much about what you an get out of God as about the conviction to affirm God and follow him umper to bumper (tailgating): okwukwe abukamaha maka ihe Chukwu a-emere gi kamahadu maka inabata ya na ikwere na Chukwudi na ndu i).

Our Challenge

As a Christian,

- Witness: let your way of life be gracious.

- Share: present and re-present your faith with sense of esteem and renewed enthusiasm to non-Christians, fallen Catholics, lukewarm Catholics, non-Catholics.

- Invite: work concretely to bring people back to church and to the life and worship of your Church community.

Seize from now to be a disinterested spectator (Zacchaeus on tree op). Become an insider and active participant in the life and work of the hurch (Zacchaeus in the House).

Remember

As we conclude this homily on Faith, remember Apostle Peter orking on the waters at the invitation of Lord Jesus (Matt 14:22-33); eter displayed faith and remained afloat, but when he disdained faith, e started sinking. Jesus Christ affirms in the Gospel that "I have come o bring fire on the earth, and how I wish it were already kindled (Luke 2:49)! This fire of Divine Love is impossible unless Christ dwells in our earts; and Christ can only dwell in our hearts through faith.

In the tide of life, are you afloat or are you sinking? Do something ow!

28. John 14:1-14

Is Your Heart Troubled?

"Do not let your hearts be troubled" – these are the very words Jesus.

Friend, often in the Bible, we hear Jesus our Lord and Savior te us: Do not be afraid! Do not be disturbed! Do not worry! Do not I frightened! Do not let your hearts be troubled!

The reality is that sometimes we are disturbed, we are afraid, v worry, we are frightened. I, myself, am a priest. However, there are tim in my life when I have been terribly afraid, frightened, worried ar disturbed.

There is this story of a boy, Jonny, who had phobia of dark place The Mother had noticed this and wanted to end the phobia. One da while she was cooking, she smartly asked little Jonny, who was in tl kitchen with her, to go and bring her a can of tomato sauce from tl storeroom. Displeased, Jonny, who had no audacity to refuse after tl mother had assured him that Jesus was in there and would keep hii safe, grudgingly and slowly left for the store room. Jonny, however, d not enter the storeroom because the place was dark. Instead, he stoc outside the lighted corridor and shouted: "Jesus, if you are in ther would you please hand me a can of tomato sauce?"

So, the truth and the reality is that from time to time we can becon afraid, disturbed, frightened and worried.

But what is Jesus actually saying when he tells us: Do not be disturbe do not be afraid, do not worry, and do not be frightened? Jesus is tellii us that in such circumstances, we must always remember that we a never alone in the journey of life because he is our "Immanuel" (Goc is-with-us). That is why we take names and give our children names as

Chika (God all-powerful)

Chima (God all-knowing)

Chidi (God is real, present and active)

Chinedumije (God leads me)

Munachimso (God is with me)

Chidumebi (God lives with me)

Chiemerie (God wins)

Chinonso (God is near)

Chigaekwu (God has the last word)

Chinaesom (God follows me)

In the last line of this gospel reading, we hear Jesus saying to us: those things that I do, you shall do even more". One of the things that esus did was that "He overcame all". And following him, believing not nly in him but believing him, having faith in him, worshipping him, VE SHALL ALSO OVERCOME!

Let us sing this inspirational song:

We Shall Overcome!

We shall Overcome!

We Shall Overcome Some Day!

Lord deep in My Heart, I do believe!

We shall Overcome Some Day!

29.   Philemon 9;9-10,12-17; Luke 14:25-33

Your Sense of Self, Family, Possession!

Hymn: Riwe ya enyela M!

Friend, in the gospel passage above, does Jesus really mean th
we should hate our parents, hate our siblings, hate spouse, hate o
children, hate oneself? Capital NO!

Jesus is simply saying that being Christians mean that we mu
work for a renewed world where a sense of self goes beyond person
fulfilments, where a sense of possessions goes beyond greed (a
untamed desire and passion to acquire and accumulate more and mo
even to the detriment of one's soul and relationship with God- jiji
nwayoo, onweghi nke ebu ala mmuo) and where a sense of family mu
go beyond blood ties. Jesus is saying that our relationship with o
another and with God is supreme to any other human longing.

This understanding informed St. Paul's appeal to Philemon (in t
reading above) as he sends poor runaway slave, Onesimus, back to h
master Philemon: "I am sending Onesimus back to you. Do not acce
him any longer as a slave, but as a brother in the Lord".

This is why we must always accept ourselves and respect ourselv
rich or poor, and recognize one another as brothers and sisters of equ
standing before God. This is why we must endeavor to treat everyo
as "persons" and not as "things" no matter how lowly placed they m
be.

This brings me to a testimony of a man who showed wonder
preference for relationship with God and people over personal fulfilme
and possessions. He is Fr. Joseph De Veuster (popularly known
Fr. Damian). He was a Belgian Missionary in Honolulu, Hawaii. H
Bishop was searching for a Priest to send to a leper settlement
Honolulu as no Priest had accepted this mission. Fr. Damian accepte
In the process of carrying out this ministry, he became so intima
with the poor lepers that he contacted the dreaded disease and died
the age of 49. His contemporaries called him names and accused hi
of imprudence and foolhardiness. But this accusation is unfortuna

nd must have come from people who were too full of themselves ecause Fr. Damian never chose to go to the leper settlement to contact prosy; he never chose to go to the leper settlement to die; he simple hose to go and serve his poor leprosy-infected brothers and sisters. he edifying end of the story is that after so many years, the Church e served and Fr. Damian's detractors came to recognize his heroic nctity and named him St. Damian the Leper.

Dear friend, continue to pursue that which you know to be good, ue and holy. Push on! And know one thing: Often the truth about us never told when we are around; the good things about us are never en when we are around. But God sees everything, and will reward ach according to his or her deeds (Cf. Revelation 22:12).

30. Isaiah 66:10-14; Gal 6:14-18; Luke 10:1-12, 17-20

Sending out the 72 on Mission: Mission of the Laity

Hymn: *Obu onye ka m g'eziga n'uwa?*

Lekwa m ziga m (dc),

M ziga gi k'ime gini?

Ka m gaa zoputa uwa na mmehie ya nile (dc),

Lekwa m ziga m.

We are soldiers, soldiers of the lord; In the name of Jesus, we sh
conquer.

Jesus affirms: "The harvest is abundant, but the laborers are few. *
ask the master of the harvest to send laborers for the harvest."

Friend, there once was a three-day workshop on evangelizatio
in a parish. On the closing day, the Parishioners were asked to con
and sign-up and make commitments to help evangelize the Parish. Th
Pastor approached a person in the Parish hall who was not making ar
moves and asked: "Would you like to go up and make a commitment
The young man replied the pastor, "No, I think that job is for the b
guns!

Thinking of this young man, winning souls for Christ is somethir
that should be reserved for the "big guns".

In the periscope of the above gospel, however, Jesus teaches ar
demonstrates that mission in the Church is indeed for every Christia
big guns and little shots alike; the clergy as well as the laity; the ordain
as well as the un-ordained. The Gospel according to Luke has two stori
of Jesus sending his followers on mission. In Luke 9:1-6 (mission of tl
12 Apostles), he earlier sends out the 12. Later in Luke 10:1-12, 17-2
(Mission of the laity), he sends: out the "72 others". Sending this latt
group sheds light on the proper understanding and interpretation of tl
words of Jesus when he says: "The harvest is abundant but the labore
are few, so ask the master of the harvest to send laborers for the harves

this episode, Jesus inaugurates the mission of the laity in the Church. This is, indeed, the commissioning of lay ministry, indicating that evangelization is not the exclusive task of the 12. The *rason d'etre* for this extension to the 72 (Jewish number for totality) is the prayer in Luke 0:2.

We have to note that the 72 were amazed at what Jesus accomplished through them (Luke 10:17: that acting in the name of Jesus, not only physical illnesses, but even demons submitted to them. How amazed the) at what they did in the name of Christ! How amazed we can become what we can achieve when we work together in the Church for the ory of God.

If all of us Christians can become deeply involved in and committed evangelization (Disciples in Mission) in our parishes or faith communities. Similar amazement awaits us in what Jesus can accomplish ough us. Working together in the Parish or Faith community (ordained d un-ordained) within our specific roles and proper ministries, we n accomplish a lot. This is an invitation, a wake-up call from God to ch of us on faith pilgrimage.

"Lord Jesus, help me to get more involved in the life and mission of e church." Can we sincerely say this prayer daily? Amen!

31.   Gen 13:8-11; 16:1-2; 17:15-17; Matt 8:18-22

The God of Impossibilities: Do not Ignore Him!

Friend, we learn from Sacred Scriptures and Sacred Tradition enrich our encounter with God. The books of Genesis and letter the Hebrews tell us about Abraham's relationship with God, and bo describe Abraham as "Our Father in Faith". We cannot think of t. Economy of Salvation or Salvation History (God establishing a spec relationship with humanity) outside of historical Abraham.

In the Bible readings above, three big lessons are drawn for us Abraham's encounter with God, which is narrowed down to the Gosp periscope.

In this encounter, we observe:

1   Abraham's Separation with his Junior Brother, Lot (Gen 13: 11):

Abram said to Lot, "Let's not have any quarrelling between you an me, or between your herders and mine, for we are close relatives. Is n the whole land before you? Let's part company. If you go to the left, *I'll* to the right; if you go to the right, I'll go to the left. Lot looked around a saw that the whole plain of the Jordan toward Zoar was well watered, li the garden of the Lord, like the land of Egypt. (This was before the Lo destroyed Sodom and Gomorrah). So, Lot chose for himself the who plain of the Jordan and set out eastwards. The two men parted compar

Let us not forget that it was Abraham that God called and promis that he will be blessed, and through him, all mankind will be blesse Abraham decided to take Lot along so that he could also share in I blessings. Sadly, we see in the turn of events the interplay of sinceri over deceit (aghugho) and selflessness over selfishness and greed (O ochucho na anyaukwu). Lot could not even oblige his senior broth Abraham the courtesy of allowing him to choose first.

An Igbo adage says: "The little child who rushes into war shou understand that death is imminent ("Nwata ji oso agbakwuru ogu, makwa n'ogu bu onwu"). Thus, we see Abraham gaining everything ev from the desolate arid land left for him while Lot lost almost everythir ncluding even his wife, from the fertile land that he had rushed to choose for himself.

Lesson: When we deal with one another in sincerity, God blesses us, but when we apply deceit, selfishness and greed, we run the risk of losing very blessing from God.

11. **Sarah and Hagar** (Gen 16:1-2):

"Now Sarai, Abram's wife, had borne him no children. But she had n Egyptian slave named Hagar; so she said to Abram, "The Lord has ept me from having children. Go, sleep with my slave; perhaps I can uild a family through her." Abram agreed to what Sarai said".

Here, do we notice that Sarah took the law into her hands. Her action mplies that since God could not do it for her, she should be allowed to o it her own way. But in doing so, Sarah created problems for herself, ost her peace of mind, and at the same time wanted to run away from he problems that her action created by sending Hagar away. But God ent Hagar back to Sarah. It was like God saying, "Hagar do not go nywhere but stay put because she has created the problem she is trying o shy away from ("Hagar igba aga ebee, lakwuru ya, o ga-ahu isi ya"). **esson**: When we ignore God and try to solve our problems our own ay by taking the law into our hands, we create lots of problems for urselves. God can allow the problems we create for ourselves to stick to s for a while.

Abraham's laughter and the God of impossibilities (Gen 17:15-7)"

"When Abram was ninety-nine years old, the LORD appeared to im and said, 'I am God Almighty; walk before me and be blameless.... s for Sarai your wife....I will bless her and will surely give you a son by er'. Abraham fell facedown; he laughed and said to himself, 'Will a son e born to a man a hundred years old? Will Sarah bear a child at the age f ninety?'"

Here, God reminds Abraham that he is the God of impossibilities. nd if he is the God of impossibilities, then we cannot at any point give p on him.

There is this story of PUSH where a man wanted a rock located close o his house moved because the radiation from the rock was becoming unbearable. He went to Jesus for this problem to get out of the way and the Lord asked him to go to the rock every day and continue to push until it gave way. The man, who was disappointed after long period of pushing without results, went back to Jesus to ask annoyingly why the rock was not moving. He interrogated Jesus: "I have been pushing but I can't move the rock! Jesus retorted: "I asked you to PUSH the rock I didn't ask you to MOVE the rock; You do the pushing, I will do the moving!"

Lesson: The meaning of PUSH in spirituality is: Pray until something happens. In whatever situation, continue to push until God responds because our God is the God of impossibilities. Never give up pushing.

In the Gospel of Matthew cited above, Jesus' talk on Foxes and Birds teaches that we should learn to entrust our security unto God and not on anything of this world. His reference to burying the dead teaches that we must continue to commit totally to God and the gospel of Jesus Christ.

Friends, let us continue to seek the God of Impossibilities in Spirit and in Truth, and with total commitment and surrender. Amen!

2.   Jeremiah 23:1-6; Psalm 23; Mk 6:30-34

Jesus Christ: The Shepherd of our lives

Friend, let us reflect on Psalm 23: The Lord is My Shepherd.

In the Bible text from Prophet Jeremiah, God made a promise to shepherd his people himself.

In the Gospel according to mark, this promise comes fulfilled in Jesus Christ.

And we have in the psalm f David 23 that beautiful inspirational prayer by which we acknowledge and proclaim Jesus Christ as Shepherd of our lives, and which summarizes what this Good Shepherd entails for us.

The greatest act of our religion, and the greatest calling of the Church and of individual Christians is Worship: Worship of God (Cf. Revelation 1-11; 5:1-14). And two of the perfect ways that we do this worship is through the Eucharistic Sacrifice and through praying the Psalms. Let me illustrate with Psalm 23 the richness of the Psalms as powerful in the worship of God:

- "The Lord is my shepherd, I shall not want": I declare God here as my leader!

- "He makes me lie down in green pastures": I declare God here as my provider!

- "He leads me beside the still waters; He restores my soul": I declare God here as my peace of mind!

- "He guides me through the right part for his name sake": I declare God here as my teacher!

- "Although I walk through the shadow of death, I fear no evil for you are beside me": I declare God here as my courage!

- "Your rod and your staff comfort me": I declare God here as my companion!

- "You spread a table for me in the presence of my foes": I decla God here as my defender!

- "You anoint my head with oil": I declare God here as my sanctifie

- "Goodness and kindness will follow me all the days of my life" declare God here as my good fortune!

- "I shall dwell in the house of the Lord as long as I live": I decla here to God, therefore, that "I am in"; am staying with Go period!

Do you see, friend, how through this Psalm alone you worship Ge as you boldly proclaim him leader of your life, your provider, your pea of mind, your leader, your courage, your companion, your defend your sanctifier, your good fortune, and you finally make a self-surrend to him in the last line?

Friend, the Psalms are divinely inspired to express our innermo feelings, and even our fears and hopes. The Psalms are powerful f worship, supplication, spiritual and physical healing, deliveranc divine guidance, exorcism and all forms of spiritual warfare. With tl Psalms, you can unlock locked doors of opportunities; with the Psalr you can shatter evil strongholds; with the Psalms you can rebuild shal foundations.

No wonder the Church has adopted and made the Psalms prominent element of her Divine Office and Eucharistic Celebratio Pray the Psalms daily; sing Psalms to God in worship and admiratio make this a commitment.

Psalm 22:3 says: "Oh my God….Thou art holy. Oh, thou who a enthroned upon the praises of Israel" (Note Israel of the NT is tl Church).

Friend, if God were enthroned upon your praises and upon tl praise of the whole Church, how glorious would He appear?

This worship, these praises, this fellowship so wonderfully render to God whenever you pray the Psalms, are best realized around tl Lord's table at Holy Mass, especially on Sundays (Cf. Acts of Apostl 2:42) rather than around the TV set.

3.   Genesis 11:1-9; Acts 2:1-11; John 20:19-23

It is the Spirit that Gives life

Friend, if you have access to the Catechism of the Catholic Church CCC), please read numbers 731, 737 and 738 on Pentecost.

It is a day of renewal in the spirit of that first Pentecost. Scripturally, :wish people celebrated the feast of Pentecost long before it became 1e feast of the descent of the Holy Spirit. They celebrated it in the :mple at Jerusalem 50days after the Passover to remember that at lount Sinai, God came down in wind and fire to give them the Ten :ommandments. This explains the large crowd present in Jerusalem 50 ays after the resurrection of Jesus. As people gathered to celebrate the :wish Pentecost, the Holy Spirit descended on the Apostles in a rushing f wind with tongues of fire.

The result of this incident reminds us of the incident of the Tower of abel in Genesis Chapter 11. In the incident of the Tower of Babel, God mfused the language of men because the believers of Babel wanted to 1ake their own part to heaven without God. It was a tower motivated by uman pride and not based on firm foundation and conviction of faith. ut at Pentecost, God reunited the languages of men as he comes down • us in the Holy Spirit, uniting all of us and all peoples into a new way f life in Christ Jesus.

Till today, the Holy Spirit has continued to gather disciples, from our rst Christian ancestors to us, their children in faith, forming us to live :cording to the Spirit of God in charity, joy, peace, patience, goodness, .ith, mildness and temperance (Cf. Galatians 5:22-23).

In the Gospel according to John, Jesus breathed his Spirit unto his »ostles and imparted peace (John 20:22). Let us recall here the Book of enesis 2:7 where the first created man, Adam, did not have any sign of fe until Creator God breathed his spirit into his nostrils. Equally, those 1arged with preaching and building God's kingdom would not have fe-giving capacity to fulfil their mission until the breath of Pentecost.

Jesus says to us again as he said to the Apostles: "As the father has sent 1e, so I send you (John 20:21); Go out, therefore, to the whole world and make disciples of all nations (Matt 28:19).

In the Nicene Creed on Sundays and solemnities, we profess faith the Holy Spirit, the Lord, the giver of life. It is through the breath of the Holy Spirit that we come alive as Christians in the world. Without the breath of the Holy Spirit, we will be "stillborn", spiritually. The life the the Holy Spirit gives to the church, she gives to all her members through Baptism, Confirmation and Eucharist (the Sacraments of Christian initiation).

Today, as always, ask God to renew in you and in the Church the Holy Spirit who is the Lord and giver of life. We again sincerely pray *Veni Sante Spiritus*, Come Holy Spirit, come into our hearts, come into our homes, come into our Parishes and renew the face of the earth make us true followers of Christ and reaffirm our faith in, love for, and commitment to Christ and his Church.

May the Holy Spirit and the Immaculate Virgin Mary who is the spouse of the Holy Spirit continue to lead us to deeper faith in Christ and sincere commitment to the Church. Amen!

4.   Micah 5:1-4a; Hebrews 10:5-10; Luke 1:39-45

We Celebrate, Proclaim and Live in the Church God's Wisdom, not Some Human Wisdom

Friend, in the Gospel of Luke 1:28, the angel, Gabriel sent from God said to Mary, the daughter of Joachim and Anna: "Hail, Mary, full of Grace; the Lord is with you." And in the same Gospel of Luke 1:42, Elizabeth the wife of Zechariah prophesied about Mary: "Blessed are you among women, and blessed is the fruit of your womb." These put together are the very words of the "Hail Mary" prayer, especially in the Rosary, that is part of our Catholic devotion.

It is very important to state that the words of this "Salutation", "Annunciation" and the acceptance changed the course of history and made it possible for God to enter human life in a visible manner. THEY ARE THE WORDS OF THE HAIL MARY. And each time we re-proclaim these heavenly words in an attitude of prayer and accept them in our hearts, God intervenes in life's events; GOD COMES… Emmanuel! There is no better time when these Heavenly words become so real to us as during Advent and Christmas time.

It is pertinent to remember the two most important persons in, and the two most important instruments of our spiritual warfare. Jesus and Mary (Cf. Gen 3:15 – the *proto-evangelium*), translate into the Holy mass of Jesus Christ and the Holy Rosary of the Immaculate Virgin Mary as two Heaven-given weapons of Spiritual assault against kingdoms of darkness.

Friend, I want you to see, then, why Immaculate Mother Mary came down from heaven in 1917, using Fatima as the locale, to urge us to continue to proclaim the Words of the "Hail Mary" for the final decimation of evil in the world.

Dear friend, in the Church what we celebrate, proclaim and live a mystery is God's wisdom and not human wisdom, "for nothing is impossible for God" (Luke 1:38), and "blessed are you who believed that what God spoke to you would be fulfilled" (Luke 1:45).

Can you now see why great testimonies abound through the centuries even in our own time, concerning the miracles God continues to work in the lives of people when the Words of the "Hail Mary", especially in the Holy Rosary, are proclaimed? I urge you: Take up your Rosary! Proclaim those Heavenly Words anew! Each day, let God continue to intervene! Let God continue to come to us! He is Emmanuel! Amen!

5. Isaiah 52:7-10; Hebrew 1:1-6; John 1:1-18

Count Your Blessings!

Hymn: Count your blessing name them one by one

Count your blessings see what God has done

Count your blessings name them one by one

And it will surprise you what the Lord has done!

Friend, can you take a minute to count your blessings?

In Bible texts from 2 Samuel 7:1-16 and Luke 1:67-79 respectively, od helped King David to count his blessings and helped Zechariah to ng the *Benedictus* acknowledging God's goodness. At Christmas, we lebrate God's ultimate blessing to humankind – the gift of His only egotten son, the infant Jesus, God made man, born for us. The gift of is son is the root and source of all other blessings. It is this gift that e acknowledge at Christmas – we proclaim it, we celebrate it, we live And the infant Jesus was given to us to see and to believe (one is of ght and one is of faith), and who we proclaim, celebrate and live, is the rince of Peace.

At his birth, he announced Peace (Cf. Luke 2:8-14); at his resurrection e imparted peace (Cf. John 20:19-23) and at each Holy Mass (Eucharistic elebration), he leads us to renew and relive peace at the "kiss of peace". et us live and work to see that the peace of the infant Jesus finds a ermanent place in our hearts, in our homes and in our Church (and not *a obu udo, echi obu agha*). We should always pray and work for divine freshment in our souls, divine peace in our hearts and homes, and ivine visitation to all our needs. Never allow the devil to make a nest your heart (*Biko ekwekwala ka ekwensu bata kuo gi akwu n'ime obi*). ontinue to strive to be instrument of God's love, peace, humility, and reconciliation which Christmas signifies.

Full of Christmas joy and blessings, may we enter the new year with earts renewed, minds transformed and bodies inebriated so that God's rosperity will continue to flow for us all "like a river" (Isaiah 48:18). men!

36.   Mark 1:12-15; Mark9:2-10; John 2:13-25

The Desert, The Mountain, The Temple

Friend, it is striking to observe that these three Gospel passages a the Gospel texts for 1st, 2nd and 3rd weeks of Lent Year B. They present tl desert, the mountain and the temple respectively. Biblically speakin these are important places of special encounter with God.

We notice from the text of John the presence of two temples: tl structure and the body of Christ. We also learn that both the temple th is a structure and the temple that is our bodies are all important to Go

Does it surprise you, then, that Jesus was so enraged that he had do what he did? The truth is that in Jesus' time, people had forgott the weightier matters of their religion to attach more importance secondary matters. In their temple worship, the Judaisers had plac rituals over and above love of God and neighbor; they were concern more with high quality cattle, sheep and doves for temple sacrifice ar exchanged dirty money for "holy temple money". Scandalous! Original every Jewish temple was designed to have five sections or courts:

- Holy of Holies

- Court of Priests

- Court of Israel

- Court of Women

- Court of the Gentiles

The temple made room for everyone, showing that the house of G(is home for all. But the Jews of Jesus' time and their priests abolished tl court of the gentiles and converted that space into "a holy marketplac for selling animals for temple sacrifice and money exchange. Tl infuriated Jesus. And by cleansing the court of the gentiles, Jesus w fighting the mentality that placed cult over people, pious religio practices over healthy human relationships.

Jesus warns us today, too, against such a mentality. Many Christia today, and indeed many who claim to be pastors, have taken the house

od, have taken the church, merely as a venue and an avenue for social
etworking and business outreach, with little emphasis on the house of
od as a place for prayer, worship, search for holiness and maturity in
ealthy human relationships:

- The way and manner people are ready to fight one another and
  gossip with one another, even at the very doors of the church,
  attests to this mentality.

- The way and manner people dress for church in utter irreverence
  to God attests to this mentality.

- The way and manner our children often behave in the church, a
  symptom that parents do not teach them proper behavior in the
  house of God, attests to this mentality. The list is inexhaustible.

Friend, an important aspect of maturity is the ability to develop
wider horizon of perspective. Be not exclusive in your human
lationships. Be inclusive; embrace all and try to see the God-image in
ery human being, no matter how deformed they may look to you.

May God's grace continue to help us strike a healthy balance between
tuals (what we celebrate) and life (how we translate and relate what we
lebrate in human relationships). This will cause our external acts of
votion to acquire relevance before God. Amen!

37. Gen 15:5-12, 17-18; Jer 31:31-34; Heb 5:7-9; Jn 12:20-3

Covenants

Friend, the covenant theme offers us an opportunity to explore t] historical development of our covenant relationship with God.

In the text from Prophet Jeremiah (Jer 31:31-34), God promis a new covenant, different from the Adamitic, Noatic, Abrahamic a Mosaic covenants.

It must be stated, however, that these covenants are interrelat in the sense that God's eternal intention for special relationship wi humankind (Divine Covenant) was seen to have been enacted in Genes 15:18-20 (Abraham), elevated in Exodus 24:8 (Israel), perfected in t] Pascha of Luke 22:19-20, and personalized at Baptism. The *rason d'et* according to the Scriptural text of Hebrew 5:7-9, is that humankind c share in the glory of God (Cf. Philippians 3:17-4:1). The proof of effica is the Transfiguration (Cf. Matt 17:1-8; Mark 9:2-8; Luke 9:28-36).

This new covenant of Jeremiah has been fulfilled through the passio death and resurrection of Jesus Christ. The blood of the new and etern covenant has been poured out for us and for many.

Through our baptism, confirmation and reception of Euchar (Sacrament of Christian Initiation) we have appropriated it and becon participants in, and beneficiaries of this eternal covenant, i.e., we ha entered into the life and mission of Jesus Christ.

In this context, the Scriptural text of Hebrew 5:7-9 reminds us th Jesus, the mediator of this new and eternal covenant, learned to ob through suffering: he obeyed God in both fortune and misfortune. I did not disobey God even in suffering; rather in all situations, he offer up prayer and supplications with cries and tears, to the one who is ab to save him; and he was heard!

This is a roadmap for all believers in Christ: we are called to be prie: (ministerial or baptismal) with Jesus, and after his example. We are n to allow hardships and sufferings to affect negatively our mindse thoughts, and actions; or worse, move us away from God – NO! T] divine summon is that we do not conform ourselves to the patterns is world, but strive to be true citizens of heaven (Cf. Philippians 3:17-1).

Even going further, in the Gospel text from John, suffering and eath acquire a new meaning and significance in Jesus. While for any, suffering and death constitute an interruption in their lives and ission, for Jesus, suffering and death fulfill his life and mission: "The our has come for the son of man to be glorified" (John 12:23). By citing e Parable of the wheat, Jesus flatly refuses to seek any help, human or ivine, to prolong his earthly life beyond his father's will.

Jesus reminds us that nothing should come between us and the love f God, and even mortal death should not frighten us any longer because e no longer conform to the patterns of this world but have been remade the image of Heaven. As children of the covenant, let us continue to ek the things that are above, for "whoever serves Jesus must follow im, and where he is, there will his servant be" (Cf. John 12:26). Amen!

38.   2Kings 6:8-17; Matthew 17:1-9

The Gift of Spiritual Eye, Supernatural Sight

Friend, we have our physical eyes, our natural sight. With th
we can see and judge things the natural way, the worldly way. But
Baptism, God infused in us another type of eye and sight: the spiritu
eyes, the supernatural sight. With this, we can see and judge things tl
supernatural way, the heavenly way.

In this biblical text of 2 Kings 6:8-17, the king of Aram was at w
with the people of God, Israel. But before each war, Israel would kno
the war tactics of the Aramites and deploy counter tactics to defe
them. The king of Aram was told that Elisha was revealing all his pla
to Israel using his prophetic powers. The king of Aram, who had becor
infuriated, deployed his troops to go and capture Elisha. When Elish
servant discovered that they had been surrounded, he ran to Elisha
panic and said: "Oh my Lord, what shall we do?" Elijah, who was n
ruffled, replied: "Do not be afraid, those fighting for us are more th
those fighting for them". With the mountainside covered with advanci
troops, the servant would not believe Elisha; he could not reconcile wh
Elisha said with what his physical eyes and natural sight showed hi
Therefore, Elisha prayed to God for his servant and said: "O Lord, op
his eyes that he may see". God opened the servant's spiritual eye and ga
him the gift of supernatural sight. And what did the servant see? He sa
the hills full of horses and chariots of fire all around Elisha. The invadi
army was humiliated by the God of Elisha.

This story also helps us to understand what took place at tl
transfiguration (Cf. Matt 17:1-9). Jesus was already helmed from eve
side. His Apostles were down-spirited because of the impending doo
Peter was already using his natural eye to evaluate the situation (Cf. M
16:13-23). But Jesus had to rebuke Peter: Go behind me, you thing t
natural way, the worldly way, and not the heavenly way.

Just as Elisha needed God to give him a spiritual eye, supernatu
sight, to his servant, Jesus also needed to give to the Apostles the sar
to give them a glimpse that God's abiding presence was still with him.

Friend, you must look beyond your condition at any point in tir see what God in Christ is doing in your life. God is always at war for s heritage, the apple of his eye, his own possession, and that is you and That is why God continues to invite us to repent of our sins and come ack to Him (Ps 51; Phil 2:3; Titus 2:11-12; I Cor 6:18-20), to believe im and have faith in Jesus Christ (1Jn 5:4-5).

Each of us must continue to ask God to renew our gift of spiritual es and supernatural sight; only with this can we see and judge things e heavenly way. Without this gift, the Christian runs the risk of being sily overwhelmed and overrun by momentary and temporary setbacks life. We need the strength of our spiritual eye and supernatural sight remain focused, to push on and to win our spiritual battles.

Believe God! Believe God! Believe God! The servant of Elisha lieved in Elisha. But he did not believe Elisha because he could only e the invading army, but could not see God's horses and chariots of e shielding them from the enemy. The Apostles believed in Christ, but ey did not believe Christ until their spiritual eyes were activated at the ansfiguration.

May God refresh your anointing to see events in our life and in your mily, in the church and in the world in a heavenly way. May God move u from carnality to spirituality. May you be heaven-bound and not rth-bound. May you see deep and believe: believe God, believe Jesus hrist, believe the Holy Spirit, believe the Church.

Let us pray: Lord, in the events and difficult circumstances of my life, ve me spiritual eye and supernatural sight to see what you would want show me. Amen!

39. Ex 24:3-8; Lk 19:11b- 17; I Cor 11: 23-26; Mk 14:12-1(22- 26

The "Pulpit" and the "Table"

Hymn: N'Oriri Di Aso...Eligwe n'uwa na emekorita...

Friend, the "Pulpit" and the "Table" have been present with us in t Church of Jesus Christ for over 2000 years from the time of the historic Jesus. And none of the two will ever disappear in the Church until Chr comes again. The Catholic Church remains a celebrating Church that built on the Word and the Sacraments.

Jesus Christ instituted the Pulpit of the Word. Listen to the Gosp according to Mark 16:15: "Go into the whole world and proclaim t good news to every creature."

Jesus Christ also instituted the Table of the Eucharist in the upp room (Cf. Luke 22:7-20). Listen to Luke 22:17-20 as abridged: "...e this is my body.... this is my blood.... Do this in memory of me."

The Table is not only a historical reality, it is a living reality: Just Jesus reclined at table with his 12 Apostles over 2000 years ago, ea time we hear these words echoed, Jesus Christ is active and prese through the voice of the Church. It is Christ the Head addressing us, I Members, directly. And when Christ said, "Do this in memory of me" is a timeless invitation to celebrate this Sacrament of his body and bloc the Eucharist. This is what the Apostle Paul emphatically recalls in wh seems to be the oldest account of the institution of the Eucharist (C 1Cor 11:23-26). If we can recall here the Post resurrection Eucharist th the Risen Christ administered to "Cleopas and the other disciple" (C Luke 24:13-32) and how Jesus disappeared from them after that, we s the Risen Christ establishing another mode and level of relationship a communion with his disciples, with us from a Historical relationship a Eucharistic relationship. Jesus Christ, risen and alive, wishes that ea of us become a Eucharistic person (ahu gin a obara gig a n'si eucharis eucharistia), while endeavoring to approach the Eucharist with decoru and decency (Cf. 1Cor 11:28-30; 1Cor 10:14-22). An emphasis about t Eucharistic table etiquette for all Christians invites us in these Scriptu exts to always remember that we are also Body of Christ (anyi nile bu ut ahu), a mysterious union-encounter where the "Mystical Body of Christ" receives the "Sacramental Body of Christ".

One of the greatest sins a Christian can commit against the Eucharist is to discriminate in the Church (iro out n'ime nzuko Kristi bu aru). Those who are in the habit of discriminating and isolating people in the Church should stop sinning against the Eucharist in this manner before they are thrown into God's prison because of this sin. And do you know what God's prison is? It is divine isolation: when you are divinely isolated, you dry up, you become a dry bone. Do not allow it.

Misunderstanding might come up at times. It is human and normal. But we must be on guard, vigilant, so that our misunderstanding does not degenerate into something demonic and causes a terrible disaster, be it in the family, in the Church or in the community. What starts as a small misunderstanding, if not checked, can snowball into unimaginable calamity. The graduation can be slow, but it can become huge: from misunderstanding (nghotahie) to quarrel (nkuko) to dispute (esemokwu) to resentment (mkpomasi) to bitterness (obi ilu) to murder (igbu ochu). Do you see how what started as a joke can become demonic (resentment, bitterness, murder) if we are not on guard, vigilant? May the celebration of the Pulpit of the Word and the Table of the Eucharist continue to purify our bodies, minds and hearts and bring us to union with Christ and unity and genuine friendship with one another. Amen!

40. Acts 15:1-2,22-29; Rev 67: 2-3,5,6,8; John 14: 23-29

The Church Defines Our Faith, Not the World!

Friend, in the text of revelation, Apostle John, while exiled in tl Island of Patmos, has a vision of the Holy City coming down fro heaven, and in this Holy City, God dwells among men. In this vision Apostle John the coming to be of the Church of Jesus Christ on earth underscored. Jesus Christ is the head of that Church; the Holy Spirit the Sanctifier of that Church; and we are the Members of that Church

Acts 15 present us with the first Pastoral Council of this Church he in Jerusalem and the outcome of that Council. Though Apostle Pet was the head of the Apostolic College, Apostle James presided over th council and moderated it in order to address a doctrinal and pastor issue.

Through the centuries of Christianity, it is the Church that h always defined our Faith based on the teachings of Jesus Christ, found on the Holy Scriptures and Holy Tradition, and sensitive to the signs the time. It is the Church, precisely the Catholic Church that defines o Faith according to Gospel values and principles. It is not the world th should define our faith according to the values and spirit of the worl NO!

In the Scriptural text of John 14:23-29, the Holy Spirit, imaged the Advocate, the Teacher of truth, the Sanctifier, the Principal age of Evangelization, has always helped the Church to perform this divi assignment from generation to generation. Pentecost was not to be time-bound event. The promised Holy Spirit that came upon the Apostl and the Church is for all times and all ages. And the Gospel preached Jesus Christ, the Apostles, and is still preached to us today, remain Go News. It is Good News because it brings God's blessings, the fulfilme of his promises and eternal salvation.

But to bring about all of these, this Good news must first challen us and the way we live, and the Holy Spirit must anoint our hearts a souls.

Friend, I would ask you to read CCC 739 and 747. Those who have t pirit of Christ in them will always accept the Gospel and its challenges, nd thus enjoy the blessings that the Good News brings. But those who ave the spirit of the world will always take up arms against the Gospel nd the agents of the Gospel, and perhaps end in self-destruction.

In the Gospel, Jesus Christ imparts peace and promises the Holy pirit. Let us pray for that peace which the Holy Spirit brings into our ouls that enables us to live according to the Gospel of Jesus Christ nd remain obedient to the Church, as the contrary would only lead to elf-destruction. Let us continue to seek the intercession of the Blessed 'irgin Mary, who is the spouse of the Holy Spirit, the queen of Apostles. et us help Christians in order to remain faithful to the deposits of faith. men!

41.   2Sam 7:12-14a; Rom 16:25-27; Luke 1:1-38

Divine Plan versus Human Instrument

Friend, in the text of Romans 16:25-27, Apostle Paul invites us celebrate the great mystery known only to God for ages: God becomin man. We also see in the Gospel according to Luke 1:1-38 that tl human instrument for the realization of this eternal mystery is Mar This became possible with her "Fiat" (Yes Lord). But to say this "ye was not without some anxiety and feeling of uncertainty on the part Mary. This was because to be the mother of God was not a light matt Though it seemed difficult, he relied on the God who never deceives, ar salvation came to the world.

The implication of Mary's "Yes" for us is that God's invitation in tl various circumstances of our lives has lasting consequences for the li and wellbeing of others. (oku Chineke n'akpo anyi n'otu n'out uboc abuna ubochi nwere uru o n'abara mmadu maka nzoputa ma anyi n'a chukwu ofuma). That is why a positive response to God's will becom decisive for the salvation of all. Look at the generations of those wl sought and did God's will: Abraham to David to Joachim and Anna Mary and Joseph to the Messiah. What do we see? We see a God wl keeps faith with the generations of those who love him (Exodus 20:6).

Let us join Apostle Paul in glorifying God for the wondrous thin he has done for us by sending us his only begotten son, incarnate of tl Holy Spirit and born of the Virgin Mary.

May our spiritual disposition as we journey in faith though li conform to that of Mary: "Here I am, the servant of the Lord, let it l with me according to your word" (Luke 1:38). May Christ continue to l born into the sanctuaries of our hearts. Amen!

2.   Amos 8:4-7; 1Tim 2:1-8; Luke 16:1-13

Wealth and Power (Authority)

Friend, wealth and power (authority) are gifts from God. But when ıe finds oneself in position of wealth and power, how should one ᵗhave?

In the Bible, Jesus goes hard on attitudes to these gifts and not on e gifts themselves. In the Gospel text, Jesus continues to indicate to his ᵢntemporaries (as to us today) that their understanding of, and attitude wealth and power must change for the better. He continues to indicate at wealth and power are not ends in themselves; they are means to ı end. Furthermore, the end is responsibility to God and service to ımanity. If not seen and approached in this way, both wealth and ᵢwer can become monsters. When wealth and power become ends in emselves, there is abuse of them, and the poor suffer (Cf. Amos 8:1-7). ıt when they are approached as means to responsibility and service, ᵢople are enhanced, their welfare is protected and their wellbeing sured. Jesus asks us to approach these gifts from God, not as an end, ıt as means to realize our responsibility towards God and our vocation be our brothers' keepers. In this way, wealth and power can become our instruments of salvation and channels to Heaven. In the Gospel ᵢriscope of Luke 18:18-23, do you remember the question the rich ᵢung man asked about eternal life? Do you also remember the answer at Jesus supplied to him? Do you remember what his reaction to the ιswer was?

The rich young man of this story had two things to offer to this world: ᴵigion and material wellbeing. Was he forthcoming? He was willing to ᵉer religion but ready to default in the other.

Again, in Luke 10:31-37, we read about the Parable of the Good ᵢmaritan. This parable is at the heart of the Christian massage. It ᵢminds us that our love for God must always be demonstrated through ır commitment to the wellbeing of others. This is more so for persons ᴴo are placed in positions by God wherein they can turn things around ᵣ good in the lives of people around them: in the family, in the society ᵈd in the Church. And this is why 1Tim 2:1-8 is asking us to pray and supplicate especially for our kings and rulers, and all in authority, so th they may continue to make better the situations and conditions throu which men and women come meeting with the God of Jesus Christ w makes all things new.

We pray that in the family, in the civil society and in the Churc wealth and power may always be approached and dispensed accordi to the mind of God and in a humane sense. May wealth and power the hands of people become the instruments of God, the channels blessing for all. Amen!

3. Sirach 3:2-6,12-14; Col 3:12-21; Matthew 2:13-12,19-23

The Holy Family

Friend, the family is a place to pray, to love, to care, to smile, to relax and to thank God for the gift of life. I still remember this traditional family night invocation prayer we learnt from childhood and which was stuck to my *medulla oblongata* refusing to leave me. It is that prayer through which we invoke the presence and intercession of the Holy family of Jesus, Mary and Joseph:

Jesus, Mary and Joseph, I give you my body and soul

Jesus, Mary and Joseph, help me at the hour of death

Jesus, Mary and Joseph, that I may sleep with you, and rest with you heaven

Two central messages stand out when we think of the Holy family of Jesus, Mary and Joseph. The vertical is the gift of the infant Jesus born for us so that we can participate in God's life; the horizontal is the invitation to share God's gift of life and love with one another. It is about living and loving.

The gift of the Holy family becomes a model for all Christian families participating in God's life and sharing God's gift of living and loving. It is a model for all families because it is a family rooted in God; it is a family where each member cares and is cared for; it is a family where each member loves and is loved; but it is also a family that has had its own dose of trials and difficult moments (poverty, flight into Egypt and the pain of exile, the loss of a child for three days). The Holy Family overcame all these trying moments in love because love surmounts all problems.

We pray that all families will enjoy the blessings and graces of God as they strive to live in harmony and peace and as they endeavor to overcome all difficulties in love. Amen!

44.   Acts 15:1-21
The Voice of the Church

Friend, reform from within has always been the way of the Churc even in the first generation Church. This text presents to us the fii Ecumenical Council of the Church, which took place in Jerusalei Though Blessed Apostle Peter was the head of the Apostolic Colleg Blessed Apostle James headed and moderated this council, whi issued a Pastoral Letter on some issues and challenges of the Chur at that time.

It will be nice for us to underscore and hear the bold, firm, ai decisive voice of Apostle James echo in the Council chamber:

"It is my judgment, therefore, that we ought to stop troubling t gentiles who

turn to God, but tell them by letter to avoid pollution from ido unlawful marriage,

the meat of strangled animals, and blood…." (Acts 15:19-20).

The Church must always have a voice. And this voice resides wi the Papacy and the college of Bishops. Through the papacy and Colle of Bishops, the voice of the Church remains alive and eloquent in t world

George Weigel (an American author, political and social activi distinguished senior fellow of ethics and public policy cent founding president of the St. James Madison foundation, an alum of University of Toronto and University of St. Michael's College, ai from Baltimore) has this to say about the Church and her role in t world:

"World leaders see the flow of history in terms of interes alliances, and power. Intellectuals of international repute percei humanity in terms of their philosophical, historical, or scienti theories. Leaders of great commercial enterprises analyze the wor in terms of markets to be penetrated and exploited. World-renown entertainers imagine their audiences in terms of the emotions th ek to invoke. Popes...see the whole picture: the entirety of the uman drama, in both its nobility and its wickedness. And they see through the prism of humanity's origins and humanity's ultimate estiny. Therefore, the chair of Peter affords its occupant a unique iew of the human condition, unlike that offered to any other global gure from any other vantage point".

45.   Acts 27:1-44

Being God's Instrument At All Times

Friends, in this text, Blessed Apostle Paul, a prisoner for Christ, an about 276 other prisoners were being taken to Rome on board a sh from Alexandria when a "Northeaster" storm struck, endangering th lives. The ship was so endangered that the captain and crew consider throwing the prisoners into the sea to save the ship. Paul fought to sa the lives of the helpless prisoners and warned that if the crew did as th planned, they would all be destroyed. He reassured the people in the words: "I urge you now to keep up your courage; not one of you will lost" (27:22); "Keep up your courage men. I trust in God that it will tu out as I have been told" (27:25); "I urge you, therefore, to take some foc it will help you survive; not a hair of the head of any one of you will lost" (27:34). After these words of encouragement from Apostle Paul the endangered shipmates, Paul had the calm, tranquility and serenity celebrate Holy Mass in a wrecking ship. He never lost his demeanor. Pa at this moment of trepidation, must have remembered God's promis and clung unto then: "Do not be afraid" (Matt 14:27). "Not one of t hairs of your head falls to the ground without God knowing about (Luke 21:18). "I will give my angels charge over you in all your way (Psalm 91:11).

Friend, do you see how Paul sustained about 276 through a sh wreck? He became God's instrument for others in a helpless circumstanc

If there are times when we must stick to God's promises, it is wh things seem hopeless and helpless. Salvation, healing, redemptio deliverance, is about getting up from the mess and moving forwa to God who stands right in front and inviting as he did to Peter in t storm: "Come, it is I. Do not be afraid" (Cf. Matt 14:22-33).

5.   Sirach 15:15-20; 1Cor 2:6-10; Matt 5:17-37

Freedom of Choice & Responsibility

Joshua ben Sirach (who lived 180 years before Christ) teaches on freedom.

Friend, in the "land of the free and home of the brave, Sirach's First reading reminds us that freedom defined as right to choose comes with responsibility. The text reminds us that God does not understand freedom or liberty as license to do whatever one wants (Is 15:20). In other words, whatever are your choices, you should be ready to accept the present and eternal consequences as they come to you.

Apostle Paul in the Second Reading adds that practice of freedom of choices should go with that maturity that God's wisdom brings.

Jesus emphasizes in the Gospel that our freedom of choice must always be guided by Christian maturity. This attaches importance to the interior state of our minds and consciences, especially concerning issues purity, decency, truthfulness, honesty and justice. Jesus pins the whole message of today on love: that we must love others so much that we don't want to harm them. We must try to live according to the mind of Christ, who also has won us this grace of practice.The truth is that whenever we feel we are smarter than God and decide to follow our own rules as Adam and Eve did in Genesis, we face disaster.

However, we must be careful not to condemn ourselves when negative feelings come into us, such as anger, envy, greed, pride, lust, laziness. How we respond to these negative feelings or instincts is what important to God and to our salvation. --Mmiri g'edoriri (the rain must come), Ide Mmiri g'ehuriri (the flood must flow), but we channel the flood so as not to enter the House and do damage. So it is with our negative feelings and instincts.On the Readings of today, CCC 1972 says: "The New Law is called a *law of love* because it caused us to act from the love infused by the Holy Spirit, rather than from fear. It is a *law of grace* because it confers the strength of grace to act, by means of faith and the sacraments. It is a *law of freedom* because it sets us free from the ritual and juridical observances of the Old Law, inclining us to

act spontaneously by prompting charity. Finally, it lets us pass from t
condition of a servant who "does not know what his master is doing"
that of a friend in Christ…."Let us pray to live this law of Christian Lo
this law of Redemptive Grace, this law of Responsible Freedom eve
day and in all situations - Amen.

We Are the Lord's: No Room for Wrath and Anger!

Hymn: Abu M nke Jesus, otu obula osiri di, abu M nke Ya mgbe le...

Friend, in the text from the Letter to the Romans, Blessed Apostle Paul asserts emphatically: "WE ARE THE LORDS".

What do you really mean when you affirm: "I belong to Jesus!"? How do you understand it?

As children of God, as followers of Christ, even as human beings, we are always filled with a sense of bewilderment whenever we read the above text of the Gospel of Matthew on the story of the unforgiving attitude of the ungrateful servant.

Is it, then, surprising that the text from the writing of Ben Sirach (who lived 180 years before Jesus) warns: "Wrath and anger are hateful things. Yet, the sinner hugs them tight"?Many children of God, many christians today, harbor malice and raging anger against one another. Do not let anger lead you into sin. The sunset must not find you still angry. Do not give the devil a foothold" (Eph. 4:26-27).

How does the devil come in through anger? He comes in through a graduated chain of action, which begins in a subtle way: from Anger (Iwe) to Misunderstanding (Nghotahie) to Quarrels (Esemokwu) to Dispute (Nkuko) to Resentment (Mkpomasi) to Bitterness/Bitter spirit (Obi Ilu) to Murder (Igbu Ochu).

Murder (whether through the use of external weapon or through our mouth), begins therefore, in a very subtle way.

Let us always remember the words of wisdom from Ben Sirach in the text above: "Remember your last days, set enmity aside". We all need forgiving and clean hearts so that evil thoughts and actions and feelings and instincts do not becloud us and prevent our prayers from getting to God and attracting his mercies and blessings. For "Blessed Are the pure in heart. They shall see God!" (Matt 5:8).

I invite you, dear reader, to sincerely look back: The above Gospel

passage on the ungrateful servant makes one strong point: If you do n
share God's forgiveness and love with others, you lose it! We rememb
9/11. We take a look around our world: wars, terrorism, militanc
kidnapping, armed brutalities, civil unrest, street and neighborhoc
violence; and we see the harm that resentment and bitterness has do
and can still do to humanity, and we ask: who will be the next victim?

For the promises and blessings of God to actualize in our live
we must renounce and forsake sinful heart (love and fancy for sir
unbelieving heart (nothing God's moves it) and wicked heart (think
talks and acts evil of others) – Cf. Hebrews 3:12-13. Animals fight ar
minutes after fighting forget it and move on to playing together. M
God give us all the grace to forgive the injuries which human actio
or inactions have inflicted on us, individually and collectively. May H
grace help us to overcome man-made walls of enmity and barriers
genuine Christian love. Amen!

8.   Isaiah 7:10-14; Matt 1:18-24

Blessed He Who Does Not Lose Faith In Me!

Friend, in the Scripture passage from Prophet Isaiah, God rebukes the people of Israel for being weary of the Lord, i.e., losing patience with him.

One may ask: why shouldn't the House of Israel be weary with God? Must they have waited for 42 generations before God could fulfill his promise to send them the Messiah to bring light to their world that had been in darkness? (Cf. Matt 1:1-17).

But the truth is that they had no alternative to waiting patiently for the Lord to act. For act He will: He is always faithful, and only He, God, can do it.

Luke 1:45: Blessed is any person who believes that what was spoken by the prophets will be fulfilled. Faith entails Patience with God for him to do it, and confidence that he will surely do it.

Friend, in our relationship and dealings with God, we must always hope for the best no matter the situation, no matter the circumstance, no matter the trials and temptations. This is Faith. This is the practical signification of "Immanuel: God is with us" which we read in this Gospel of Matthew.

Friend, ask for the grace to be submissive to the will of God, for what He has in stock for you is better than whatever you may wish for yourself and whatever you can imagine for yourself. I pray for God's graces upon you as you move through the years ahead. Amen!

49.   Mark 9:2-10; Matt 17:1-12; Luke

Every Glory Comes With a Prize

I want to use the Transfiguration event of Jesus with the Apostles address our Youth and Young Adults particularly.

Friends, one thing we learn from the transfiguration of Jesus, recorded in the gospel, is this statement that "Every Glory (Succe comes with a prize". In the account of the transfiguration drama, wh the Apostles witnessed was so delightful to them that Peter exclaime "Lord, it is good we remain here. Let us make three tents, one for yc one for Moses and one for Elijah". They had never seen something li that in their lives. But Jesus gently replied: "No, not yet! We must down and pay the price first".

Friends, it is always good to dream big: I want to be an astronaut want to be a Neuro-Surgeon, I want to be an Architect, I want to be Medical Doctor, I want to be a Soccer or Football Superstar, I want to a Celebrity, I want to be a Priest, I want to be a Nun, etc. But it is anoth thing to be ready to pay the price to get there, which is hard work.

Many people are dreaming big every day and are working hard realize their dreams. This combination of the glory and the prize mak these people dynamic, resilient, focused, and religiously/spirituall morally/intellectually sophisticated. But there are many other you people who are almost disappointing, who are not measuring up (dare I say, lazy), who feel they ought to have been born with "a silv spoon in their mouth". These are the very ones who, accidentally becor dropouts and a nuisance to their families, to society and to the Churc

Dear Youth and Young Adult, remember always: Big dreams a achieved with hard work. And you can only work hard when you avc undue distractions, bad friends and unhealthy habits.

May you continue to grow in wisdom and in the knowledge of Gc Amen!

). Mark 9:2-10; Romans 8:31b-34; Gen 22:1-2, 9a, 10-13, 5-18

Life on the Mountaintop and Life in the Valley

Friend, let us look at the Transfiguration of Jesus from another angle. The spontaneous response of the Apostles to this incident was that they wished to remain on that mountaintop. But Jesus rather ked that they go down to the valley. This reveals to us the two sides ' life: Life on the mountaintop and life in the valley. Let's take it that e on the mountaintop represents the beautiful things in our lives, hile life in the valley represents the ugly things in our lives. This is w, in faith, we have to see events in our lives: the good, the bad and e ugly.

The question is: How do we deal with both sides of life events? ur vision of faith is to see Jesus manifest as much in the valley as the mountaintop. This is the only way we Christians can share in rist's Cross as well as in his glorious blessings. Look at the long ad from Abraham (mentioned in the text of Genesis) and Jesus our vior. The text of Romans reminds us: If God is for us, who can be ainst us?Let us always deepen our relationship with Christ to enable the grace to deal with our "mountaintop" and "valley" issues with ristian maturity, to purify our intentions, make deliberate efforts overcome our weaknesses and to become sincere with God so that r external acts of worship and devotion will acquire relevance and ward from God.

Remember, friend, that Christianity is a very practical "Religion". is is so because if you must ascend to God, you must begin the ascent th your neighbor; Holiness begins here because your neighbor is e step through which you ascend to God. You aspire to go to heaven. it Heaven comes to you each day through your sincere acts of love the other done for the sake of God.

Friend, resist the danger of backsliding in your spiritual life either cause of your "mountaintop glories" which have entered your head your "down in the valley crosses" which have brought despair and sillusionment with God. Remember that none of us is yet perfect,

and we can never be perfect until we become perfect in heaven. The
is room in each of us for improvement because God is not finish
with us. It is not yet done until it is done. In every life circumstan
May Jesus Christ, our redeemer and Sanctifier, continue to uplift yo
spirit. Amen!

Luke 22:14-2356; Daniel 3:8-24, 91-97

"Father, Into Your hands I Commend My Spirit"

Friend, this prayer of Jesus, I think, is one of the most important prayers r any Christian. This prayer, from this Gospel text, depicts total surrender, tal abandonment, and total trust in God. And this is what Christian life all about: entrusting everything about us and our affairs to the hand of od.

Friend, do you know that this all-important prayer of Jesus is from the alms (Psalm 31:6)? – "Into your hands Lord, I commend my spirit"; and e very next line of the verse says: "And you will redeem me, faithful God".

The full meaning of this prayer, which Jesus understood so well and aches us to understand, is that God's redemption is right there in the oment of surrender, especially when faced with the turbulent storms of ily Christian life. This total surrender of Jesus in the face of his Cross minds us of Daniel's Shedrach, Mishak and Abednego. When faced with e wrath of Nebuchadnezzar, this trio committed their spirits to God, and od redeemed them from the burning furnace

"Into your hands I commend my spirit; You will redeem me, Lord, ithful God" This type of spiritual energy which Jesus displays, and which e trio of the book of Daniel vividly exemplifies, is what we need today be faithful disciples of Jesus Christ in the world and to be faithful to the ospel in mission. We need to display in our day a lot of spiritual energy the spiritual energy that enables us to be true to Christian principles and nvictions without default in the face of the Cross, submitting totally to od's care and power to deliver us. We need to witness more. To the Jews ho were attacking him, Jesus said: "If you do not believe what I say (that I n Son of God), believe it because of the work that I do" (John 10:38).

Friend, what we do defines who we are! In Acts of the Apostles 11:26, e notice that by the life that the first generation Christians lived, the gans in Antioch named them Christians (Followers of Christ). I think, as ristians, we should be talking less and doing more. May the Holy Spirit ntinue to help us. Amen!

52. Mark 14:1-15:7

Holy Week with Jesus!

Friend, Passion (Palm) Sunday captures for us, in a nutshell, t events of Holy Week. We must always reflect on how the events of tl week play out in our individual lives: "For if we partake in his passi and cross, we will share in his resurrection and new life".

Let us situate the events of the Paschal Mystery in our individu life stories: How does the drama of the life, passion, death a resurrection of the Lord Jesus play out in your Christian life?

What happened?: We see love in the life story of Jesus but a disappointment, frustrations and betrayal.

His human response: We see pain and sense of abandonment.

His spiritual response: We see resignation to God. Jesus mt either resign to God and his will, or throw in the towel and call it qui We all know the choice he made and the road he took. Do you cal quits with God and even going to Church (killing hope) or do y resign to Him who has the power to save you (keeping hope alive)?

His Crown: We see resurrection and glorification.

Friend, in all the events of Holy Week, we have a lot to learn, pick, to treasure. We have spiritual energies to draw from for our ov life ordeals. "Whoever wants to be a disciple of mine, let him take his cross daily and follow me." May we always remember the Gos dialogue today between Jesus and Peter:

Peter: Though all may have their faith in you shaken, mine w never be!

Jesus: Amen I say to you, Peter, this very night before the co crows, you will deny me three times (Matt 26:33-34).

Friend, each Triduum (Palm Sunday to Easter Vigil), we gatl in worship to re-enact, to re-new, to re-energize our covenant of lc relationship with God, and further cement this very love that n controls us.

During the Holy Week, as we participate in the incredible richness
the Liturgy and reflect on the dialogue between Jesus and Peter,
ay we continue to strengthen this journey of love (call it apostolic
llowership), may we continue to intensify this leaning on God's
ms (call it trust in divine providence), may we continue to brighten,
rough grace, God's eternal light that guides and guards our souls,
ır Church, and our world. May we, indeed, become more committed
the expression that our faith must find in our social life, in our
ılitical decisions, in our cultural engagements and in our economic
tivities. Amen!

53.   Is 52:13-53:12; Hebrews 4:14-16, 5:7-9; John 18:1-19:42

A) Good Friday: Our Good Fortune!

Friend, exactly this time last year on Good Friday something happene Andrea, the wife of my friend Rashawn, put to bed a bouncing baby g named Francesca. I told Rashawn, when I got the news, that Good Frid has brought his family good fortune. I was asking him again this afterno if we are expecting another good fortune today, Good Friday, one year aft

However, that incident points to us the message of today's celebratic Good Friday, our good fortune!

But let us look at the Passion of the Lord Jesus which we commemor and relive this day every Good Friday from four perspectives: **The Enign The Challenge, The Invitation and The Warning.**

The Enigma: Try to look at the days building up to the Passion, a the whole of the Passion drama: the plots, the conspiracies and the hostilit of the Jewish nation against Jesus. We are often baffled and appalled at th difficulty and struggle to understand the Person and Mission of Jesus.

But wait a minute. Do we not have the same difficulty and strug trying to understand the mysteries of Christ revealed in the Churc Let's take the sacraments, for example: Baptism, Confirmation, Euchar Confession, etc. The truth is that no person can understand the Myster of God and his ways except by the grace of the Holy Spirit. That was w the Apostles/Disciples left everything and followed him.

May the grace of the Holy Spirit continue to deepen our appreciati of the mysteries of our salvation and our appreciation of how God opera in our daily lives.

The Challenge: When we speak of the passion of Jesus, we usua mean the suffering, humiliation, torture and death inflicted on Him. E **the passion is not just something done to Jesus by others; it is als power within Jesus:** His passion is power that enables him to face violence, pain and death for our sake. Jesus has great passion in his he that consumes his whole person and drives him through this time rror and excruciating pain. He could have avoided going to Jerusalem day, especially as he knows the ultimate end of this journey. He could ve compromised and settled for survival. But the passion in his heart for r salvation is greater than his need for survival and security. Jesus is so ssionate that his passion and love insists that he faces the ultimate test of ve: the Cross.

But wait a minute: How passionate are we for our faith? What level of crifice are we ready to make for our faith in him and for love of him and hers?

May the spiritual strength and moral power that Jesus gives us through s passion sustain our faith, hope and love.

The Invitation: When faced with pain, disappointment, andonment and betrayal, Jesus resigned to God's will: "Not my will but ur will be done" (Matt 26:39); "Father, into your hands I commend my irit" (Luke 23:46).

When faced with pain, disappointment, abandonment and even trayal in life, do you throw in the towel and call it quits with God and e Church? Do you give up and give in (killing hope)? Or do you resign to od (keeping hope alive)? Jesus did the latter, and it paid off!

May our "Kiss of the Cross" this Good Friday be one of continued love r Jesus, his kingdom and his Church. May this Kiss not be one of betrayal Judas Iscariot did.

The Warning: Remember the dialogue between Jesus and Peter.

Peter: "Though all may have their faith in you shaken, mine will never ".

Jesus: "Amen I say to you Peter, this very night before the cock crows, u will have denied me three times".

What Jesus is telling Peter and us is: Look, the implications of our faith e not tested here in the four walls of this room/church, but out there hen we step out. It is out there in our social interactions, in our political cisions and choices, in our cultural engagements and in our economic tivities

As Jesus asked his Apostles "Let us go" when "the die was cast", I now ggest to you, friend, in the name of Jesus Christ, "Let us go".

May we continue to have the spiritual courage, confidence and boldne to follow Christ. And may spiritual timidity, despair and fear not be o portion – Amen!

B) Good Friday: The Cross and The Sacrifice

Friend, every Palm Sunday and Good Friday in the Gospel, Jesus pra the Psalm 31:6: "Into your hands I commend my Spirit…. You will redee me Lord, faithful God". On Good Friday, in fulfilment of Psalm 69:22, Jes takes the "sour wine" (vinegar) for our sake, for our sins.

There is this hymn in the Igbo language that essentially captures t Holy Week Spirituality: "So Gi ka M g'eso rue ogwugwu, na ndu m nile, ka M g'ebeku Nna, ihe Gi ka M g'eso rue ogwugwu, obula na uzo mma gbaa ochichi (translation: "I will follow you Lord to the end, all the da of my life, I will continue to lean on your everlasting arms. Your light w continue to guide me till the end. Even if the ways of humans turn dark, t way of God is everlasting light").

Holy Thursday is the celebration of the Lord's Supper, Good Friday the celebration of the Lord's Passion and Holy Saturday is the solemn Eas Vigil: all move us towards this everlasting light of God's abounding love f all.

The texts from Prophet Isaiah, letter to the Hebrews and Gos according to John shed light on "the Cross and the Sacrifice". The Cro and the Sacrifice won pardon for our offenses and brought us salvatic As people of the Cross and the Sacrifice (evidenced in our veneratic of the cross of Christ), God invites us to be more determined to take Christ's work of bringing God's love and mercy to our world, as individu Christians and in the community of the Church. As people of the Cro and the Sacrifice, let us be ready always to bear the crosses that faith a life would place on our shoulders, and let us be ready to make the sacrific that faith and life would demand from us for the good of all. Let us witne more with our lives, share more of our faith with others and do more invite people back to God's love made available in Christ and accessil through the Church.

Friend, may the mysteries of God in Christ that we celebrate a receive give us the much-needed spiritual energy to stand for Jesus Chr in today's world. Amen!

4. Acts 10:34a, 37-43; Colossians 3:1-4; John 20:1-9

A) Halleluiah: Rejoice, Christ is Risen!

Hymn: He's alive, Amen, He's alive, Jesus is alive forever, H's alive men…

Psalm 118:24 of Easter Sunday invites all Christians throughout the orld to Rejoice. Why Alleluia? Why do we rejoice?

Friend, we rejoice and sing alleluia because this day, Christians all ver the world mark this event making our faith and "Religion" unique, ecial and quite different from all other religions of the world; that Jesus hrist, the founder and cornerstone of our faith, truly died and truly rose ;ain on the third day, a fact of history. No other founder of any religion ed and rose again on the third day, and no other Religion claims this.

This means, my friend and fellow Christian and pilgrim, that we are tablished on a sure path to salvation and eternal life. This is why we joice. This is what we celebrate each year at our "Christian Passover": at salvation and eternal life is a blessed assurance for all who accept sus, "for all who live and die with Christ will rise again with him to ewness of life" (Cf. 2Tim 2:11-12). That is why we proclaim every ister night (which is the mother of all nights) the *Exultet* (Nuribanu), well as the three solemn proclamations of the Alleluia (the song of e redeemed), before the Paschal Candle: That in Christ, our victory is sured. "Who can conquer the world? Only he who believes that Jesus the son of God" (1John 5:5).

The Evangelist, John, tells us: "We are witnesses to all these before u so that you may believe, and having believed, you may have life rough him" (John 21:24). This is the truth we celebrate and rejoice in Easter, and this truth is immortal. People can suppress it, accuse it, ndemn it, torture it, kill it, bury it in a grave; but on the third day, truth ill rise again.

Napoleon Bonaparte, a military and political leader during the latter irt of the French Revolution, said at the end of his life: "I know men and ell you that Jesus Christ is no mere man. Between him and every other rson in the world there is no possible term of comparison, Alexander

the Great, Caesar, Charlemagne, and I have founded empires. But (
what did we rest the creation of our genius? Upon force. Jesus Chr
founded his empire upon love; and at this hour, millions of men wou
die for him". Napoleon, therefore, asked for a crucifix to be placed on h
chest when he dies; and that is why you see a crucifix on his chest whi
lying in state.

Friend, do not give up on the truth. Hold on to it, even when tl
world around you would have it otherwise. Hold on to the truth th
Christ has won, and we know that in Christ, we shall overcome somed
halleluiah. Praise the Lord!

Continue to stick to the Lord; Continue to stick to your faith in Hi
Continue to worship Jesus Christ arisen in His Church. Amen!

B) Hell Will Not Let Loose On You!

Friend, Happy Easter! May this joy, won for us over 2000 years ag
continue to be yours forever, and may you continue to share in t
victory of Christ's resurrection in all your life circumstances. On Goc
Friday, it is all woe for Jesus: his good friend, Judas Iscariot, betrays hi
his trusted companions, the Apostles, desert him; His number one m
(Peter) denies him twice. The people that he so much loved demand h
crucifixion and prefer to have Barabbas, the notorious, freed instead.
is as if Hell had let loose on Jesus.

But three days later, he arose! He conquered death and sin. Pain a
sorrow gave way to victory and joy, and the power of God triumph
over evil.

Friend, you are the child of Easter. No matter what you are goi
through now, does this scenario speak any message to you, to yo
situations and circumstances, to your pains and agonies? Your victo
over evil belongs to Jesus Christ in whom we trust. Today, Christ h
won. And in Christ, we shall continue to overcome. Halleluiah!

Friend, this brings me back to that psalm that Jesus prayed on Go
Friday (Psalm 31:6): "Father into your hands I commend my spirit; y
will redeem me lord, faithful God". Sing along with me: "So Gi ka M g'e
rue ogwugwu, na ndu m nile, Gi ka M g'ebeku Nna, ihe Gi ka M g'e
rue ogwugwu, obula na uzo mmadu gbaa ochichi (translation: "I w
follow you Lord to the end, all the days of my life, I will continue to le

your everlasting arms; Your light will continue to guide me till the d. Even if the ways of humans turn dark, the way of God is everlasting ht". Amen!

Friend, Child of God, direct beneficiary of Christ's triumph over sin d death, continue to strengthen this journey of love we have all begun Christ, continue to nurture and treasure God's love that now controls r lives, and continue to be faithful on our sure path to salvation.

55.   Gen 28:10-19; Matt 1:20, 2:13; 1John 4:1-6

Dreams!

Friend, let us examine in depth this very important issue as it rela'
to the practice of our faith today.

What is a dream?

A dream is a series of images, pictures, sensations, thoughts a
images that can occur when a person is sleeping or seemingly sleepir
or during certain stages of sleep.

Who or What motivates dreams?

A) God -- also called Godly (true) dreams or Heavenly dreams:

Numbers 12:6 – "Hear now my words: If there is a prophet amo
you, I, the Lord, will make myself known unto him in visions and w
speak to him in dreams"

Job 33:14-15 – "For God does speak, perhaps once, or even twi
though one perceives it not. In a dream, in a vision of the night wh
deep sleep falls upon man".

B) Satan/ Devil (*satana/diavolo/demono*), also called devilish
satanic or false dreams. The devil does bring terrifying dreams:

Ecclesiastes 5:2 – "For nightmares come with many cares"

Job 4:12-13, 16 – here Satan gave Eliphaz a false dream for job.

Satan, being a fallen angel and a spiritual being (whose powers we
not removed) can also appear to us in dreams or initiate dreams
manipulate our faculties and influence our dreams.

In dream experiences that generate fear, sickness, anxiety, otl
adverse effects or even mysterious deaths, it is recommended that o
who goes through this should seek Divine intervention, healing and,
deliverance.

C) Our Psychological/Emotional/Physical states: This is anotl
source of dreams, also called illusion or illusive dreams.

Do dreams occur?

We, ourselves are living examples.

We have two classical examples from the Old and New Testaments:

Genesis 28:10-19: Jacob's ladder and God's blessings. This came true (Bethel: House of God).

Matthew 1:20: (Joseph): "Such was his intention when, behold, the angel of the Lord appeared to him in a dream".

Matthew 2:13: "Rise, take the child and his mother, flee to Egypt, and stay there until I tell you. Herod is going to search for the child to destroy him".

Is any person immune from dreams? No!

Can dreams come true? From what we have seen from the Sacred Scriptures, is sometimes, yes, and sometimes, no.

What should be our Christian reaction?

"Echekwubela na nro means what?

- Pray and hand over to God whatever you see in your dream. He has the last word.

- If the dream portends good omen, claim it in Jesus name; And if it portends bad omen, cancel and reject it in Jesus name.

- Above all, 1John 4:1: "...test every spirit whether they are of God".

Exhortation: Be courageous, be bold in the face of dreams, especially, when such dreams portend bad omens. Do not allow the devil to use bad dreams to outdo you with hysteria (grave fear) as this can suffocate your spirit.

Friend, let us continue to pray for healing; for deliverance from devilish, satanic, demonic dreams. Let us pray, too, for the cancellation of the terror from such dreams on us and our people. Amen!

56. Exodus 24:3-8; Hebrews 9:11-15; Mark 14:12-16, 22-2

Corpus Christi: "Blessed are those called to the Supper of the Lam

Friend, our Church, the Catholic Church, is a celebrating Chur founded on the Word and the Sacraments. Through the year, we a either celebrating a Solemnity, or a Feast, or a Memorial, or an Option Memorial or Feria.

The readings, here, celebrate the Solemnity of the Most Holy Bo and Blood of Christ, popularly called *Corpus Christi*.

Friend, sing along with me: **N'oriri di aso, Enigwe n'uwa emekorita, Chukwu na mmadu aburu otu, ndi no n'eligwe na n no n'uwa emekoria bie oma, buru otu n'ime mmuo, oru ebube, o itunanya, Chineke bu amamihe n'onwe ya, ihunanya ya ebukakw umu mmadu kelenu Chukwu: doo Nna ekele diiri Gi Chukv (Translation: In the Holy Eucharist, Heaven and Earth come togeth in fellowship. God and Man become one. Those in Heaven and tho on Earth become spiritually bound. This is a miracle; this is awesom God is wisdom himself. His love is inestimable. Children of me thank God: Oh Father God, receive our gratitude).**

In the Reading from Exodus 24:3-8, Moses takes the Book Covenant and proclaims it aloud to the people: At Holy Mass, Chr our High Priest takes the Book of the Covenant *and* proclaims it alo to his people. This is what is called, during Holy Mass, **"The Liturgy the Word"** which concludes with the Creed and Prayer of the faithful

In the same reading again from Exodus, Moses takes the Blood the Covenant and sprinkles the people and says: "This is the Blood the Covenant": At Holy Mass, Christ our High Priest takes his Ov blood (not the blood of bulls or goats or calves that do not have power obtain salvation as underscored in the reading from Hebrews), and sa "This is my blood, the Blood of the new and Eternal Covenant, whi will be shed for you and for many, for the forgiveness of sins". This what is called, during Holy Mass, **"The Liturgy of the Eucharist"** whi concludes with Communion Rite.

By receiving the Body and Blood of Christ, we become part of tl ody; we become part of that blood. We become, indeed what we eat nd drink. This is why Pope Pius XII in the encyclical, *Mystici Corporis Christi,* describes us, members of the Church, as "the mystical body of Christ", i.e. Through the Eucharist, we express what we are as Church. This mystical union between us and Christ through Eucharistic communion expressed symbolically (in signs) when, before consecration, the priest drops a few drops of water into the wine, and as he does this, he prays: By the mystery of this water and wine, may we come to share in the divinity of Christ who humbled himself to share in our humanity".

Friend, be reminded that we come to participate at Holy mass fundamentally to be part of Christ's invitation to receive His Holy Body and Precious Blood, for "Blessed are those called to the Supper of the Lamb".

Many Christians give reasons why they would not come to Holy Mass to respond to Christ's invitation: The Mass is boring; Priests don't preach good homilies; those who go to Mass are hypocrites; Priests give communion to so and so who is unworthy; and so on, excuse, excuse, excuse. We have heard them all. **But those who give all those human-based excuses ignore what God is doing at Holy Mass.**

"Blessed are those called to the Supper of the Lamb". Friend, when you and I received our first Confession and first Holy Communion, we began to respond to this invitation. May we continue to approach the Eucharistic Jesus with devotion, reverence and sense of adoration continue to enjoy that divine refreshment in our souls, that divine peace in our hearts, and that divine visitation to our needs, which the Eucharistic Jesus brings. Amen!

57. Numbers 11:25-29; James 5:1-6; Mark 9:38-43, 45, 47-48

"Our Promised Land" and "The Land of Promise"

Friend, let us place our various nations before God. In the spi of Numbers 11:25-29, no one person no matter how well-intention can bring any country or nation to the promised land of their drea it is the responsibility of all stakeholders. In the spirit of this Scriptu passage also, we must continue to commend the "Moses" of our natio (The Commander-in-chief) and "the 70 elders" of our countries (tho working with the Commander-in-chief: Governors, ministers, tl executive councils, the legislative councils, the Judiciary) to God. This because the Scripture passage from the Apostle James 5:1-6 reminds that when God raises one up and gives one an exalted position in socie one should use it to make the lives of the people sweet and not to increa their suffering that leads to gnashing of the teeth. Our leaders have to this remembering, according to the Gospel passage from Mark chapt nine, that good deeds come with blessings (ihe oma n'eweta uru) and b deeds come with misfortune (ihe ojoo n'eweta oghom).

Friend, many countries have had leaders vested by God wi authority and power. For most countries, it has been a tale of the goo the bad and the ugly in governance. Many national leaders who me well for their countries at the start end up becoming confused, distracte manipulated, eliminated or outright despotic. That is why, piecing tl three scripture passages above together, we must continue to pray f good governance and work against greed and corruption in society. various countries, their peoples know their histories, their achievemen and their setbacks as a people. No outsider can tell these better th they can. Common setbacks in our world today include but are n limited to civil unrest, violence, wars, terrorism, militancy, kidnappin armed robbery. There are also some good signs at grass-root governan and restoration of the confidence of the people in Government. O responsibility is to participate in the task of restoration because we a all in it together. How do we participate? By praying for and showi good will towards our various countries; by contributing to provi education and infrastructure in our families, villages, neighborhoo ommunities and states; by enlightening and influencing our peoples to e positive about their countries; by showing through our actions that e are a clean and descent people and by avoiding modes of behavior at can portray our countries in bad light to outsiders.

Friend, if you are person yelling that his or her country is not orking, then, the questions arise: How selfless are you? How much o you work harmoniously with others? How much do you love your untrymen and women? How ready are you to work for collective als and shun individual "ego-project? With your exposure, travels, lucation (you name it), are you sure you have become better in your entality, choices, temperaments, appetites and inclinations than others ith lesser opportunities?

Friend, nothing is wrong with our countries. Many things are wrong ith us. God is willing and ready to lead our countries to their earthly romised land, as well as lead all of us individually to the land of Promise Heaven. But we all need conversion, patriotism, re-orientation, commitment and rededication towards what is good, true and just for e common good. Our prayer is to see our various countries thrive, rosper and succeed in our life time. Amen!

58.   Acts 9:26-31; 1John 3:18-24; John 15:1-8

Respecting Order, Recognizing Gifts and Building Up th Church

Friend, in the Post-Resurrection Liturgy, the Church presents the fir generation Christian Community to teach how they lived and identifie with the mission of our Supreme Master and Lord, Jesus Christ.

In this biblical text, Paul's mission was genuine because he receive his Apostolic calling through a direct revelation from the Risen Chri However, his mission could have lacked legitimacy if Paul had not mae effort to identify with the Apostles/Disciples and indeed integrate h ministry into the missionary activities of the early Church. Thus, he ha to travel to Jerusalem to meet with the elders of the Church.

Lesson 1: One's zeal for God's work should not lead one to tI illusion that one can operate independently of the Church of Chri or, worse, make our ministry self-styled. Many self-acclaimed "zealot have fallen into this illusion, and this has left Christianity in fragmen' Every person wants to be Bishop or Archbishop; every person wants be priest; every person wants to answer "His or Her Grace", "His or H Eminence", "His or Her Holiness".

Lesson 2: The Apostles, after some initial disquiet, welcomed Pa and recognized the gifts the Risen Christ has given him. We and o Church leaders must be more open to the gifts of the Holy Spirit th abound in the Church, and recognize and accept such gifts. While v must accept that some people left the Church because of their untame ambition, we must also take some blame for some who left because our failure to recognize and accept their God-given gifts.

If we are able to harmonize both in the Church: Individual Christia on the one hand, recognizing that their gifts lack legitimacy unless communion with the Church, and the Church Community, on the oth hand, recognizing individual gifts for ministry and building up t Church, the Church throughout the world will know peace and will built up (Cf. Acts 9:31)

Lesson 3: What about building up the Church? At one of our Bil udy sessions in the Parish on Thursday, April 19, 2013, during which e study topic centered on "Supporting the Church", a participant said is in her contribution: "The Vatican should sell all those treasures in e Vatican and use the proceeds for the work of evangelization and stop king for collections". As the moderator of the Bible study, I asked her vo questions: Have you been to the Vatican? And how much of those easures you speak of did our own generation put there? (Guess the iswers).

Friend, from the time of the first generation Christians to the present, e Church of Christ has, indeed, continued to develop in times of peace id in times of affliction, through the operations of the Holy Spirit and rough men and women of faith and spiritual vision. Most of what we ijoy today, even our Christian faith, are fruits of the sacrifices made by any in the past.

Friend, what sacrifices are we ready to make today for the Church to ntinue tomorrow? We must not be mere consumers in the Church; we ist also become producers. Christianity is a very practical religion: no crifice, no Christianity.

Friend, don't forget: You aspire to go to heaven. But heaven comes to u each day through those genuine acts of charity to others and to the urch done for the sake of Christ.

However, we cannot do the above if we are not united "as a vine anch is united to the Vine tree" (John 15:4) or if we do not "remain him" (1John 3:24). This unity with Christ is realized, among others, rough constant contact with the Word of God, through unceasing ayer, through regular Confession, through worthy reception of the charist and through holiness of life in word and deed.

Friend, may the words of this homily open the doors of your heart d fill it with blessings, and may the Eucharist which you receive open e eyes of your mind to recognize and follow Christ more faithfully and vently. Amen!

59. Luke 13:10-17; Luke 19:1-10

Refuse To Accept That Bad Condition!

Friend, the Book of Numbers 23:19 makes us understand the eternal truth that God is not a man that he should lie. His plans and purposes for us cannot be thwarted or diverted by any other force or power.

Sing along with me this song that captures this truth:

"I bu Chineke I bughi mmadu,

I bu Chineke I bughi mmadu,

Mmadu n'ada ada, mmadu n'agharipu,

I bu Chineke I bughi mmadu,

Okwu Gi nile bu eziokwu

(Translation: You are God, you are not man; Man falls and changes. You are God, you are not man. All your Word is true).

In the first part of the text of Luke 13:10-17, prior to the healing of the woman with the flow of blood for 18 years, we see human nature at work in the Synagogue Official: He announces a timetable for God. Funny. Often in our humanness, we tend to hold God to ransom; we hold him hostage/captive; we try to determine for Him when, how, where, and even for whom He should work or not work. We even try to subject God to space and time.

But God is not man that any person should think of controlling him. God has his plans and purposes for each person He brings into this world. However, we always see in the Bible how the Devil would always attempt to derail this plan, just as he tries to do in the life of the woman who has been sick for 18 years and who has come to encounter Jesus.

The condition this woman found herself in for this length of time was not part of God's plan for her: "the enemy has done this" (cf. Matt 13:28). How the Devil had this type of power over her destiny, I do not know. It is clear from the Sacred Scriptures that evil forces

n wish to thwart God's plans and purposes, yes, but not without our
operation. However, the important lesson is that Jesus intervenes to
claim this woman's destiny because, in faith, she refuses to accept
at condition and goes to Jesus before whom all other powers and
incipalities must bow (Philippians 2:9-10).

Friend, refuse today to accept whatever bad conditions that afflict
u as your portion. Do not resign to that condition; resign to God,
ther, and come to Jesus for a turn-around.

In the text of Luke 19:1-10, we read again about Zachaeus. This
also an individual who refuses to accept the negatives about his
e: poor public image, misjudgment of him by the public, ostracism,
d unimpressive physical stature. He does not allow all these to
scourage him from going to Jesus. And good for him, Jesus ignores
e judgments and opinions of the local populace and reaches out to
chaeus to restore him to God's plan.

Woah! That woman with the issue of blood refuses to accept her
ndition, and this short man Zachaeus refuses to accept his condition.
th of them ran to Jesus, and their wounded destinies were healed
d restored.

James 4:6 through 10 says:

"But God has something better to give....Give in, then, to God and
sist the Devil and he will flee from you.... Draw close to God and he
ll come close to you.... Humble yourselves before the Lord and he
ll raise you up".

Friend, begin to reject your bad conditions now; come running to
sus for a change; declare all negative conditions as not your portion:
nful life, sickness, backwardness, joblessness, marriage and family
sputes, etc.

Declare God as your portion and ask Jesus to begin changing your
uation for good: Jesus, touch my life today, touch my marriage and
mily today, and change my destiny and the destiny of my family for
od. God, Jesus, Holy Spirit: Change my condition from sinfulness
holiness, from sickness to health, from bondage to deliverance,
m poverty to wellbeing, from war to peace, from death to life, from
rkness to light, from lack to abundance, from sorrow to laughter,

from curses to blessings, from breakdowns to breakthroughs, fra closed doors to open doors.

Declare with me, friend, that "In the Name of Jesus Christ, by t Power of his Most Precious Blood, and in the authority of his wor all these blessings have come true in your life. Amen!

). Joshua 5:9a, 10-12; 2Cor 5:17-21; Lk 15: 1-3, 11-32

Two Different Home-Bound Journeys

Friend, the Book of Joshua and the Gospel according to Luke esent to us two different journeys toward home, two home-bound urneys; the first journey, of a people or nation Israel, and the second urney, of an individual, the prodigal son.

In our journey of Faith, we often begin it as a people (having en born into the Church), but we sustain it as individuals, as each rson works out his or her salvation. Salvation is a free gift from od to all, but attaining it is not easy at all.

Israel journeyed from a nation of slaves to a nation of free people, om being under the yoke of Pharaoh to being in loving and intimate lationship with God, and from eating manna and quell in the desert feasting on the fruits of the Promised Land. In the course of this urney, the people of Israel often blamed God for their woes and umbled against him.

The prodigal son, on the other hand journeyed from being lost being found, from being dead to being alive. In the course of this urney, the Prodigal son has the credit of accepting responsibility r his woes rather than blame everyone else.

Friend, the text of 2 Corinthians talks of transformation to the w. In Joshua, the journey **transformed a nation**, Israel, to God's ople (*Kahal Yahweh*). And in Luke, the journey **transformed a art** into an abode of God.

Friend, often in the course of our history as a people or as dividuals, we may tend to blame God for our ordeals and for aatever unsavory that befalls us. But if we can, as the prodigal n did, throw away shame and pride and look inwards, we might scover that "ihe n'eme anyi si anyi n'aka" (we are, to a greater part, sponsible for our misfortunes).

However, God's love still seeks our transformation, re-creation, circumcision of our hearts by his grace. Let us always rejoice that, God's children, we are ever privileged to share in God's love. May we, who are people of God, members of his Church and citizens heaven, continue to work hard for our individual salvation using t spiritual riches of Christ that abound in His Church. Amen!

1. Acts 14:21-27; Revelation 21:1-5a; John 13:31-33a, 34-5

Jesus Designs a Uniform for His Followers (Christians)

Friend, there is a mad crave for identity in the world today: Each person thinks, how can I appear unique, distinguished, classy, or even special? For many, this crave is satisfied in putting on special outfits, uniforms, caps, headgear, staff or working sticks, etc. They feel these items single them out from others and make them appear exclusive. The situation has almost become like "Fuji House of Commotion". Think of Clubs, cultural groups, the Chiefs and Lolos, the Nze-na-zos, Knights, etc. These are not out of place, one would say. But the problem may be putting emphasis in wrong place.

In this text from the Gospel according to Apostle John, Jesus also wrestles with the question of how to design a uniform for his followers distinguish them from non-believers. His prescription, however, goes much further and deeper than external "show-show" outfit. For Jesus, the essential difference between Christians and non-Christians would not be in the way they dress outwardly, but in the way they live inwardly: "I give you a new commandment: Love one another. As have loved you, so you also should love one another. This is how all will know that you are my disciples, if you have love for one another" (John 13:34-35).

Friend, Love is our Christian identity, our Christian uniform. If you are wearing this uniform of love, then you are in. If you are not, then you are out. One person says: I love my neighbor. Another person says: I love my ice cream. Are two the same? No! One is of the heart; the other is of the taste buds.

Catechism of the Catholic Church (CCC) numbers 1970 and 1842, however, teaches: We cannot love genuinely without the Holy Spirit. In order words, the gift of Christian/Sacrificial love is not something you acquire as you would acquire a skill; it is something you receive from the Holy Spirit; it is a gift and it is given. Without the Holy Spirit, our love can become counterfeit, camouflage, mere pretense and deception (Ochi-abu-uto). We must continue, therefore to ask the Holy Spirit for the transformation of our hearts and mind

Friend, note that in the text from the book of the Acts of Apostle Paul's statement was one made from a heavy heart: "It is necessary f us to undergo many hardships to enter the Kingdom of God" (Ac 14:22). Remember that earlier in Acts 13:48-52, Paul and Barnab were attached in Antioch in Pisidia, an attack and uprising that w insinuated by influential women and leading men of the city amo whom were worshippers. They were beaten and pursued out of t city well up to Iconium. Friend, this type of insinuation and uprisii still happens in faith communities of the Church today. But Christia ought always to remember the words of Jesus before he suffered ai died: "It is written that the son of man must be betrayed, but woe that person through whom…it could have been better if that pers were not born".

Friend, whoever tries to destabilize the Church of God receiv his or her punishment from God. In love, we must all be builde of the Church, builders of our faith communities and collaborate in mission, and shun and avoid those arguments, those mentaliti those temperament, and those instincts not borne out of Christi love that turn us into destroyers of the Church and unhealt competitors in mission (Cf. Mark 9:33-37). This has harmed or ev destroyed some Church communities.

Friend, may the love that comes from the Holy Spirit as g continue to make out of us, builders (and not destroyers) of t Church of Jesus Christ. Amen!

2. Exodus 17:8-13; 2Timothy 3:14-4:2; Luke 18:1-8

Prayer Is the Master key!

Hymn: Prayer is the key, Prayer is the key, Prayer is the master key,

Jesus started with Prayer and ended with Prayer,

Prayer is the master key.

In the text of Exodus, we see Moses praying for the victory of Israel. e also see the People doing the unimaginable just to keep prayer wing in order to assure victory. But Moses did something in addition: sent his men to the field, to war. He did not just say: "look, I have ayed, let God come down and act for me".

In this incident, the Word of God underscores two important points out our prayer warfare:

First, the indispensable need to pray constantly for our needs without sing heart because there is no other short cut/option. This incident monstrates that one must explore all possibilities within one's reach remain constant in prayer or sink. Even after victory is assured, we ust remain constant in prayer to sustain our gains. The clear message this passage of the Scripture is: **Continue praying and be victorious; op praying and be destroyed. When prayers go up, blessings come wn!** Friend, you have a choice. And this covers all segments of prayer arfare: individual prayer as well as Community, or liturgical prayer. oly Mass is the Christian's supreme prayer because at Holy Mass, Jesus offered to the father (Cf. I Corinthians 11:26). The fact of life is that individuals, our hands of prayer can become weak and go down. hen this occurs, the Church Community at worship with you supplies cclesia supplet).

Second is the undeniable fact that we must match prayer with action. e must take the necessary human actions that augment our prayers. e must be realistic in praying. For example, if a man prays to God to ve him good harvest in the next harvest season but spends the whole anting season on gambling, neither clearing the farm nor planting any ed, how does his prayer materialize? If a youth or young adult prays God to make it possible for her to become an engineer, or a medical doctor, or a neurosurgeon, or a religious, or an architect but spends l time for studies on street-loitering, partying and all forms of bad hak and bad company, how does her prayer materialize?

Friend, I would like to refer you to the Miracle of the Five Loa and Two Fishes in the Gospel according to John 6:9-13: When you p: to ask for any favor, God wishes to see how far you are ready to go w him. What God sees in your palms, he blesses unto abundance. ' your palm", here, means your commitment, your involvement, and y(readiness to move with God in doing the right thing.

In the Gospel text of Luke, the widow presents her needs to Je. in prayer, but also confronted the unjust king and demanded justi Again, we see fervent prayer and necessary action highlighted as age of human transformation.

Friend, God continues to assure us that as long as we have living fa in Him, as long as we are ready to allow God to be God in our lives a not play God ourselves, He will continue to hear our prayers and give justice. But he also wishes that our prayers for divine intervention m always be supported by our good and appropriate human interventic taken to enhance our destiny. Our faith must be a creative faith and nc dormant or lame duck faith. And our readiness to renounce sinful hea (love and fancy for sin), unbelieving hearts (nothing God's moves yo and wicked hearts (thinking/talking/acting evil of others) constit viable ingredient of living faith and effective prayer to God (Cf. Hebre 3:12). Within these considerations, we ought always to pray and not l(heart as Jesus admonishes in the first verse of the Gospel text of Lu Prayer expresses our hope and nourishes our faith.

Friend, may God make us strong in our faith, unwavering in our h(and persistent in our prayer. May we always hold onto God's promi because we are also children of Abraham in Jesus Christ descended fr(David (Cf. Matt 1:1-16). In the spirit of St. Paul in the letter to Timot may we remain faithful to what we have learned and believed.

Can you form the habit of saying these two "twenty-second" pray first thing in the morning and last thing before you sleep at night?

MY FIRST MORNING PRAYER AT WAKING"Lord God, a thank you for my life and for this new day, I unite myself, my intentic and my entire family to the sacrifice of our Lord Jesus Christ on 1 ar of Calvary present on the altar of Holy Mass this day in the Church roughout the world. I also unite myself, my intentions and my entire mily to the Psalms of oblation, worship and thanksgiving being offered God this day in the Church throughout the world. And I unite myself, y intentions and my entire family to the Holy Beads of the Most Holy)sary of the Immaculate Virgin Mary through her intercession, asking at I and my entire family be covered in the holy mantle of her motherly otection forever. Amen!

MY LAST PRAYER BEFORE SLEEP

"Lord God, thank you for the day that has rolled by and thank you r this night. Put sweet, peaceful, tranquil and refreshing sleep into y eyes, as I now commit my body, heart and soul into your hands for fekeeping. May your Holy Spirit take full control of my sleep this night. 1d may your holy Archangels and Angels guard our abode in peace and ive far away from this abode all the wickedness of the enemy, that we ay sleep in peace and calmness, refreshed, strengthened and renewed rise up to newness of new day to continue to love and serve you and live in your presence forever. Amen!"

Prayer composed by:

Rev. Dr. Judethadd Osunkwo

(for private circulation only)

63. 2Samuel 5:1-3; Colossians 1:12-20; Luke 23:35-43

A) Is Christ The Universal King Reigning?

Hymn: Jesus Christ Nwa Chukwu, Okaka.

Jesus Christ Nwa Chukwu, ekele diri Gi,

Jesus Christ Nwa Chukwu, Okaka,

Obu Gi bu Eze Di Nso, Daalu!

Friend, every year we celebrate to feast of Christ, the Univer King. The question is: Who or what should exercise absolute pow over our lives, and in our homes? I presume the answer from eve Christian will be Jesus Christ.

On every solemnity of Christ the King, we answer this questi and manifest to all in unison: It should be the Lord Jesus. It is t Lord!

Friend, Jesus Christ does not reign as worldly rulers and kir and lords reign: Jesus responds to Pilate "My kingdom is not of tl world. If my kingdom were of this world, my servants would ha been fighting, that I might not be delivered over to the Jews. But i kingdom is not of this kind" (John 18:36). The arena of His kingshir not defined by geography; the arena of His kingship, his lordship, I reign, is our hearts and our homes. And wherever Christ the Univer King reigns, these virtues are seen to be promoted and lived: Holin (Adimaso), Grace (Amara), Truth (Eziokwu), Life (Ndu), Justi (Ikpe-nkwumoto), Love (Ihunanya), and Peace (Udo) (Cf. Preface Holy Mass of Christ the King).

Holiness means, for us, living decent lives, having decent hom as opposed to rotten lives and homes.

Grace means, for us, being gracious and having good sense humor in our lives and homes as opposed to being bitter, angry a stoic.

Truth, for us, means absence of falsehood and pretenses (mal believe) in our lives and homes.

Life means, for us, shunning in our lives and homes any action that dangers life or cuts life short. This includes abortion, euthanasia, icide, substances that endanger life; it means recognizing God as e author of life and accepting that all lives belong to God and are in d's hands.

Justice means, for us, seeing things objectively in our lives and mes, and not from subjective position, i.e., knowing that what we or say and how we live has impact also on others around us.

Love means, for us, wishing none any harm in our lives and homes, t being resentful, not thinking/talking/acting evil of others.

Peace means, for us, gentleness in reacting to issues, and avoiding ing explosive irritable and erratic in our lives and homes.

Friend, our vocation is to share in the happiness of God; and ppiness is not something that you can buy, win or achieve. It is a t that is given to us as a result of living the life of Jesus. Let us kindle our longing to remain under God's rule, under his dominion d authority, and let us shun all false gods. In Psalm 84:11, we sing: u ubochi na be gi ka mma, karia nnu n'ebe ozo (One day in your urts, Lord, is better that a thousand elsewhere). Remember this ying: "Better for me to live in a thatched house a free person than to e in a mansion in chains".

When we reject God's influence in our lives and homes, we should t lose sight of the dire consequences. This understanding ought to ape what we desire in life, what we want to control us, and what know will give us genuine happiness and lasting peace. This is the allenge and opportunity hidden in our celebration of Christ the ng.

So friend, is Jesus Christ reigning in your heart? Is he reigning in ur home? If your response is still in the affirmative, then, the values his kingdom should continue to prevail therein in your heart and minate all business in the home.

May the Lord Jesus Christ, the Universal King, continue to be aised in our lives, in our homes, in our Church and in the world. nen!

B) Christ's Kingdom: A trait or a Compliment to Earthl Governments?

In Nigeria and other West African Countries, Christ the King celebrated with a very festive parade through the main streets of c cities and countryside. The drums roll out with the samba, bongo a flutes. And what we do as Africans to celebrate Christ as the Univer King is not far from what Pope Pius XI had in mind when he institu this celebration in 1925: "That Christ's influence must be felt, not o in private lives, but also in public domain". This rationale comes ho again to us in an era when governments and anti-religion grou would want to push issues of Faith and Religion out of public life.

Friend, the kingship of Christ is not a trait to kingdoms a governments of the world. But in the Gospel passage of Luke 23: 43, Pontius Pilate, representing world governments (the powers t be) becomes suspicious of Christ's Government – this is seen in discomforting interrogation of Jesus. True, there is difference betwe the Kingship of Christ and the kingships of the world: other kingsh have territorial boundaries but the Kingship of Christ is eternal, i Christ is King without borders; other kingdoms and kingships co and go, but the Kingdom of Christ is eternal. Other kingdoms sustained by military and economic power but the Kingdom of Chr is sustained by the power of love and truth. Yet, despite the glari differences, friend, Christ's Kingdom is not a trait but a complim to earthly kingdoms because it is the truth and love of Christ's re that give earthly kingdoms moral power.

Unfortunately, the unfounded suspicion of Pilate (which personi that latent suspicion inherent in the psyche of Government) has I many in our time to advocate separation of Church and State in or to push God and Religion out of public life.

At a Holy Mass on September 19, 2011, Cardinal Sean O'Malley the Archdiocese of Boston, USA said: "Ironically, those who advoc a strict separation of Church and State often quote Jesus' wor "Render to Caesar the things that are Caesar's, and unto God things that are God's". What they often mean by this is: "Let's lock G up in the sacristy and let Caesar call all the shots". That can be v perilous especially if Caesar happens to be a blood-thirsty ideolog ho likes to throw people to the lions".

Friend, Psalm 24:1 says: The earth is the Lord's, and all that is in it, e world and those who live in it". As Christians, we should be loyal tizens of our nations and Governments, but loyal citizens of God's ingdom, first. Let us take our world to Christ. Christ has to be king, ot just in our hearts, not just in our homes, not just in our Church, it also in our nations and in our world.

May the Spirit of Christ help us to be visible Christians in our orld. Amen!

64.   Isaiah 49:1-6; Acts 13:22-26; Luke 1:57-66, 80

Birthday of John the Baptist: What's in a Name?

Friend, the Church celebrates the feasts of "named saints" once
year on the anniversary of their deaths. It is unique to Jesus (the so
of God) and John the Baptist that we celebrate both their birth an
death. The Gospel of Luke 1:57-66 centers on the naming ceremo
(Igu aha) of John the Baptist. In the African Traditional Religio
(ATR), we have an elaborate ceremony for naming a child (Igu aha

The name, John, given to forerunner of Jesus by God even befc
he was conceived and born (Cf. Luke 1:13), means "God is graciou
We remember, here, the old time question in Shakespeare's Rom
and Juliet: "What's in a name?"

My grandfather, Osunkwo, had three sons. It took him long yea
before his wife, Nneigwe could bear him a child. He underwe
humiliations from his kinsmen and even denial of rights and privileg
because he was childless, but he kept on praying (in his tradition
ways of prayer) and hoping. Eventually, the first son came after ma
years of marriage, and Osunkwo named him, Ofonyiri/Igwe (pray
conquers/heaven gave. Ofo is a symbol of ancestral presence, author
and prayer). It did not take a long time before the second son can
and Osunkwo named him Ejikeme (patience conquers). There w
another very long waiting, but eventually, the third son came, a
Osunkwo named him, Mputam (I can now come out to my kinsm
as I have been exalted).

My father, Mputam Osunkwo, the third and last son of the
parents, has six sons: Okechukwu (God's portion), Ikenna (Go
power), Chukwunonye (God-is-with-us). Uchenna (God's wil
Chukwuemeka (God has done well) and Chidiebere (God is mercifu

Friend, why does the Gospel show so much interest in the nami
of John the Baptist? The naming of this great prophet of God buttress
three competing interests in giving a name: the family (personal), t
culture and God (creator). These three interests bring to the fore t
conflict that sometimes exist between our familial preferences, wl
culture can impose on us, and what God wills for us. How do we p

ese interests into harmony?

We see in the text that God gave this child a name, already revealed his father, Zechariah (Cf. Luke 1:13). The action of God, here, is in ne with the text of Isaiah 49:1&5: "The Lord called me before I was orn. While I was in my mother's womb, he named me…. He formed e in the womb to be his servant…." Here we see that God already has purpose for this child, and indeed for all his children even before ey come into this world. The challenge of life is to discover this vine purpose. The role of the family and culture, then, is to assist eir members to discover this divine purpose for each, and to fulfil s demands. The role of family and culture is not to frustrate this vine purpose or to try to deviate their members from it (as some mily members and neighbors of John the Baptist tried to do).

Friend, our greatness as children of God consists in discovering hat God wants us to be and the direction God has planned for our ves. We must live out the demands of this plan, this call, this direction ithout compromise, whether it be in the areas of vocation, carrier, lent or even hobby.

Friend, I have a question for you: How has God's design for you ayed out in your life? Do you feel that God's hand has been at work ur life in any way, especially in consideration of the direction your e has been going?

Friend, to evaluate these questions, I invite you to **think! Pray! nd listen!** May the Spirit of God help you to do this. Amen!

65. Ezekiel 17:22-24; 2Corinthians 5:6-10; Mark 4:26-34

Christian Father: The Mustard Seed That Is Your Family

Friend, on this Fathers Sunday, God presents us in his Word in t Gospel according to Mark, the parable of the Mustard Seed and how t kingdom of God, like the insignificant mustard seed, would grow ir a powerful institution through God's grace and the cooperation of I disciples.

On a day as this, therefore, I want to pay special tribute to so many our fathers, and indeed many of the men whom God has used to men us and to make the mustard seed of His Kingdom grow in our famil and in our homes, which constitute the "Domestic Church" (Chur Nzuko no n'ime ufo), and in our Church Communities. This grow has been a result of their unfailing generosity and unrelenting focus pillars of our families and as pillars of the Church.

On a day as this, let us also focus our minds on the encoun between Jesus and his Disciples by the Sea of Galilee. In this encoun Jesus invites his disciples to "Cast your net over the right side fo catch" (John 2:6). Let's have three things in mind here: These are "M of Galilee, and despite the unimaginable catch of fish, their worn-c net did not tear, and afterwards, Jesus invited them to an already-ma "breakfast of roasted, smoking fish and baked bread.

Friend, often there is this temptation for us to rely more on wh *we can do ourselves*, and less on *what God can do with us*. We can thi and act well for ourselves sometimes, but God thinks about and a best for us perpetually. Remember: Christ is the same today, yesterc and forever. Why am I saying this? Because I want each Father to alw; remember the words of God through prophet Ezekiel: "I, the Lord, bri low the high tree, lift high the lowly tree, wither up the green tree a make the withered tree bloom. As I, the Lord, have spoken, so will I ((Ezk 17:24).

I call upon Fathers, "Men of Galilee", "Men of the World" to tr God more as they continue to discharge this wonderful, intrigui and challenging responsibility to their families and to their Chu Communities as God warns through Ezekiel that none can do it fruitfu thout God at the center stage.

I also appeal to fathers and men in the homes for more patience d more strength of character as they continue to discharge their sponsibilities: Patience so that they do not over-motivate, and Strength Character so that they do not under-motivate. Fathers need these two order to maintain the healthy balance between goodwill for their nilies, and the right methods to make good things happen. I invite hers to strive to practice these virtues of Blessed St. Joseph, the spouse the Immaculate Virgin and foster father of Jesus: He was a humble an; he obeyed God; he revered his wife; he protected his child; he alously guarded the Church.

Friend, I often hear children talk from their nose: "Dad is stone-ed, always mad at me; mum is always kind and smiles at me, but dad esn't". I appeal to children to please always go beyond the anger on the e of either parents and try to see also the love in their hearts that seeks e best for you.

Friend, I know that no wife would want to be a widow. I appeal also wives and mothers to please continue to take good care and account their husbands as "mma nwanyi bu di ya" (the beauty of a woman is r husband).

So, on a day as this, let us celebrate our fathers and men. Without em being there for us, we are incomplete: "We love you fathers, we lebrate you, we celebrate your lives and accomplishments. We celebrate u, not only because of what you do for us, but above all, because of ho you are to us. May your remaining days be sweeter, more peaceful, ore joyful and more fulfilling. Amen!

66. Acts 2:1-11; 1Cor 12:3b-7, 12-13; John 20:19-23

Holy Spirit Helps Us Live the Life and Do the Work!

In one of my Catechism sessions for the Sacrament of Confirmatic I showed to the candidates the traditional photo of the Pentecost wh the Apostles, in the company of Mary the mother of Christ, receiv the Holy Spirit. After a consumed viewing, one of the boys exclaim "awesome". Then, I asked the same boy a simple but funny question: H many Holy Spirits do you see in the photo? He replied: "Twelve!" an burst into laughter. The boy's innocent reply may sound ridiculous. I the way many of the so-called Christians behave today, an outsider n ask if there are many Holy Spirits. One Christian wakes up from sluml and tells the world that the Holy Spirit has told him or her so and so, to be so and so. And most of the messages arrogated to the Holy Sp by these self-acclaimed Holy Spirit dreamers, visionaries, prophets, a messengers contradict themselves. And each self-acclaimed "chur founder" proclaims his or her church as the one anointed by the H Spirit.

Friend, let us say this traditional Church prayer to the Holy Sp together: "Come Holy Spirit and fill the hearts of the faithful; enkin in them the fire of your love; send forth your spirit and they shall recreated; and you shall renew the face of the earth".

When Our Lord and Savior Jesus Christ instructed his disciples Acts of the Apostles 1:4-5, 8 to do nothing until they receive the Promis Holy Spirit, we understand that, unless we are controlled by the H Spirit, we can neither live the life nor do the work for God.

In his pastoral letter on Evangelization, Cardinal Sean O'Mal of the Catholic Archdiocese of Boston, USA, invited us all to beco more involved in the evangelization mission of the Church by follow: Christ through **witness** of life, **sharing** of our faith in an explicit v with others, and **inviting** others back to the Church (No. 5). The slog for this New Evangelization, or Re-Evangelization became, "Our Fai Witness, Share, Invite". At Pentecost Sunday every year, we join c brethren all over the world to pray for a new outpouring of the H Spirit, for another Pentecost, for the renewal of the gifts of the H irit and the manifestation of the fruits and powers of the Holy Spirit our lives, in the Church and in our world.

Friend, in this time of ours when the Universal Church calls out her children to embrace the new evangelization, the Holy Spirit, the incipal agent of sanctification and mission, will need to evangelize each us, and then take us up as instruments of evangelization to others. The ongue as of fire" which rested on the head of each of Christ's Disciples Pentecost reminds us of our unity of faith and universal call to holiness d mission, and in this way share in the life of Christ and participate in s divine mission.

Friend, as we celebrate Pentecost every year and renew our spiritual ointing, do not forget the challenge Christ throws at you today: that e true test of your faith and sense of mission is not to be found within e wall of the Church building, but outside the wall in your familial d social relationships, in your economic activities, in your political cisions and choices, and in your cultural engagements.

At the 2012 Holy Thursday Chrism mass homily, the Catholic rchbishop of Boston, Cardinal Sean O'Malley, said: "After the esurrection, Christ did not need to remind his disciples of their eaknesses, but rather went ahead to give them the Holy Spirit so that, 'God's wounded healers', they may extend God's love and peace to all". d so it is between us and Jesus our Supreme Master. And he reminds in his pastoral letter on Evangelization that the presence and action of e Holy Spirit is the source of holiness, gift of grace and apostolic zeal. e spreading of the Good News to all nations is not a task that can be hieved or a goal that can be attained by mere human strength.

May the Holy Spirit of God continue to help us respect order in the urch, recognize gifts that abound in the Church, and together build our Catholic Faith. May the Holy Spirit of God help us, not to just ep the faith, but to spread it around. Amen!

67. Genesis 1:1-31; Romans 5:1-5; Matt 28: 16 -20

Trinity: Our Lives are Oriented to Community

The book of Genesis helps us understand that in our origins, wh God made us in the first place, he created us in his own image a likeness. That image becomes clearer, through the redemptive act Christ, in the injunction of Jesus in the Gospel according to Matthe 28:19: "Go…baptize them in the name of the Father, and of the Son, a of the Holy Spirit". So, it is clear that the image in which we are creat is the image of the Trinity, the Triune God: three-in-one-and-one-i three.

Friend, we start experiencing this community of life of the Trin once we are born: we cannot exist and survive without the nourishme that comes from mom, then the warmth of human relationships, fro parents to other family members to the wider human community a to the Church family. In fact, being made in the image and likeness God who is triune, we cannot enjoy the fullness of life without being p of this communion, i.e. life-in-community. Extreme individualism a way of life, therefore, does not agree with our creative and redempti anatomy. That is why it is hell not to belong, but it is heavenly to belor That is why it is hell to live with no body to love us other than our isolat selves, but it is heavenly when we love, and are loved by others.

Friend, God made us to belong. The inner nature of God, in who image and likeness we are made, is persons who, however distinct th are, totally belong to each other in one unbreakable bond of love.

There is nothing in life, therefore, that more closely reflects the real of the Most Holy Trinity than when it is expressed in genuine family li It is when we live as a family that we truly have a glimpse into the life the Father, and of the Son, and of the Holy Spirit.

Friend, as you internalize this practically, may God bless you "In name of the Father, and of the Son, and of the Holy Spirit". Amen!

3. Isaiah 22:19-23; Romans 11:33-36; Matt 16:13-20

"You are Peter!..."

"You are Peter, and upon the rock I will build my Church" (Matt16:18a).

Friend, in this Gospel passage, we are reminded again that the Church which we are members is a Divine institution. However, God continues use human beings, mere mortals, to oversee this Divine institution; and visible structures and its organization have developed progressively, and ntinue to develop through the centuries.

When Christ says: "I will give you the keys of the Kingdom of Heaven. hatever you bind on earth shall be considered bound in Heaven, and natever you loose on earth shall be considered loose in Heaven", He does t address them to Peter as a person only, but addresses it also to Peter a symbol of authority and leadership, an authority and leadership that poses in the Church. The Church is the repository of that authority of nich Peter is a personification.

"And the Gates of the netherworld shall not prevail against it" (Matt :18b)

Friend, from Apostle Peter (the first Pope) to the present Pope Francis, have had 267 Popes in an unbroken Apostolic Succession. Christ never omised that leading the flock would be easy (Cf. Matt 16:13-22; John :15-17; Luke 22:32). And so, all through her history and development, the urch, guided by the Holy Spirit of Christ, has been subjected to attacks those who declare themselves enemies of the Church of Christ, protests d betrayals by her own children, and setbacks by her own mistakes (as d uses frail human beings to oversee this Divine institution).

Friend, in all these attacks, protests, betrayals and setbacks, the only planation for her continued existence and resounding survival is the fact at as a Divine institution, the Church is guided and sustained by Almighty d himself. She remains as the One, Holy, Catholic and Apostolic Church, e eloquent voice of God in the world.

Friend, I pray that God will continue to sustain your faith and mine in Church, sustain his Church in the world and sustain the world with the chings of the Church. Amen!

69.   Philippians 2:6-11; Psalm 31:6; John 15:1-8
JESUS IS THE LORD OF MY LIFE

Friend, this quotation from St. Paul's letter to the Church in Philip simply put, means: Jesus Christ reigns supreme over all persons and ov all powers that be.

When you claim: "I am living a new life. I am born again", you a implying that Jesus has become the lord of your life.

Let us remember that the presence and action of the Holy Spirit is t source of holiness, gift of grace and apostolic zeal. The spreading of t Good News to all nations is not a task that can be achieved or a goal th can be attained by mere human strength.

At Pentecost Sunday every year, we pray for a new outpouring of t Holy Spirit, for another Pentecost, for the renewal of the gifts of the H Spirit and the manifestation of the fruits and powers of the Holy Spirit our lives, in the Church and in our world.

The Holy Spirit, the principal agent of sanctification and missi will need to evangelize each of us, and then take us up as instruments evangelization to others. The "tongue as of fire" which rested on the head each of Christ's Disciples at Pentecost reminds us of our unity of faith a universal call to holiness and mission, and in this way sharing in the life Christ and participating in his divine mission.

At the 2012 Holy Thursday Chrism Mass homily, the Catholic Archbish of Boston, Cardinal Sean O'Malley, said: "After the Resurrection, Christ not need to remind his disciples of their weaknesses, but rather went ahe to give them the Holy Spirit so that, as 'God's wounded healers', they m extend God's love and peace to all". And so it is between us and Jesus Supreme Master. And he reminds us in his pastoral letter on Evangelizati that the presence and action of the Holy Spirit is the source of holiness, of grace and apostolic zeal. The spreading of the Good News to all natic is not a task that can be achieved or a goal that can be attained by m human strength.

I say again: When you claim: Am living a New life, Am born again, it eans Jesus has become the lord of your life. Why is Jesus our Supreme rd? What is the reason for His Lordship over us? I Cor 6:20 gives the swer: because "You've been bought and paid for" with his Paschal ystery.

How do we describe this lordship that has become part of us, and which must embrace and which should exercise absolute authority over us?

Friend, Jesus Christ does not reign as worldly lords, rulers and kings gn: Jesus responds to Pilate "My kingdom is not of this world. If my igdom were of this world, my servants would have been fighting, that I ght not be delivered over to the Jews. But my kingdom is not of this kind" hn 18:36). The arena of His Lordship is not just defined by geography; e arena of his Lordship, his reign, is primarily our hearts. And wherever rist the Supreme Lord reigns, these are the signs: Holiness (Adimaso), ace (Amara), Truth (Eziokwu), Life (Ndu), Justice (Ikpe-nkwumoto), ve (Ihunanya), and Peace (Udo).

- Holiness means, for us, living descent lives and having descent homes as opposed to living rotten lives and having rotten homes.

- **Grace** means, for us, being gracious and having good sense of humor in our lives and homes as opposed to being bitter and angry persons, or stoic.

- **Truth**, for us, means absence of falsehood and pretenses (make-believe) in our lives and homes.

- **Life** means, for us, shunning in our lives and homes any action that endangers life or cuts life short. This includes abortion, euthanasia, suicide, substances that endanger life; it means recognizing God as the author of life and accepting that all lives belong to God and are in God's hands.

- **Justice** means, for us, seeing things objectively in our lives and homes, and not from subjective position, i.e. knowing that what we do or say and how we live has impact also on others around us.

- **Love** means, for us, wishing none any harm in our lives and homes, not being resentful, not thinking/talking/acting evil of others.

- **Peace** means, for us, gentleness in reacting to issues, and avoid being explosive, irritable and erratic in our lives and homes.

Having described what this Lordship that has become part of us, a which we must embrace and which should exercise absolute authority o us entails, the question for each of us is: Has Jesus Christ become the L of my life? Or is he already becoming now?

The truth is that we still have a long way to go. We must continue work sincerely to make Jesus Lord in our lives. When we reject Chri influence in our lives, we should not lose sight of the dire consequenc But if we are united with our Lord Jesus "as a vine branch is united to Vine tree" (John 15:4) or if we do "remain in him" (1John 3:24) throu constant contact with the Word of God, through unceasing prayer, throu regular Confession, through worthy reception of the Eucharist and throu holiness of life in word and deed, this understanding ought to shape w we desire in life, what we want to control us, and what we know will give genuine happiness and lasting peace.

If Jesus Christ becomes Lord in our lives, he also becomes Lord over needs, problems and over all forces that would try to torment us. He ind becomes, as Psalm 23 articulates for us: leader of my life, my provider, peace of mind, my leader, my courage, my companion, my defender, sanctifier, and my good fortune.

The prayer of Jesus while on the Cross, from Psalm 31:6, "Into yc hands lord, I commend my spirit; and you will redeem me, Lord, faith God", I think, is one of the most important prayers for any Christian. T prayer depicts total surrender to and total trust in the lordship of Chr And this is what the lordship of Christ over us is all about: entrust everything about us and our affairs to the hands of God.

Friend, fellow pilgrim in faith, the full meaning of this prayer, wh Lord Jesus understood so well, and teaches us to understand, is that Chri redemption is right there in the moment of surrender.

Jesus Christ is Lord! May you surrender completely to him tod Amen!

John 6:1-69

Eucharist: Covenant with God and With One Another

Friend, the long discourse of Jesus on His Body and Blood, a stinguishing feature in the Gospel according to John, offers us portunity to reflect on the divine invitation, the Spirituality of Holy ass and the Eucharist as covenant.

The Eucharist is our Covenant with God and with one another)riri Nso bu ogbugba ndu na agbata anyi na Chukwu na mmadu).

Friend, I hope you know the four principal expressions of the Holy ass: as Sacrifice (Aja), as Thanksgiving (Inye Ekele), as Banquet)riri Mmemme) and as Covenant (Igba Ndu).

At the last Supper, Jesus says: "This is the new covenant in my ood" (Luke 22:20) – Jesus is our covenant with God and with one other – Obara Jesus emeela udo n'agbata Chukwu na mmadu, gbata mmadu n'ibe ya.

We have the concept of Oath (Idu Isi) and Covenant (Igbandu) the Igbo Culture of South Eastern Nigeria. In Oath taking, no venant meal is involved, and peace and reconciliation are not aranteed. On the contrary, Covenant is always accompanied with covenant meal (called Oriko), usually provided by parties to the venant. In a covenant, the expected result is always peace and nuine reconciliation. Covenant has consequences: unconditional ceptance of one another, discarding of grievances, double edged ord (could be a blessing or a curse).

In Christ who is our covenant, we have entered a covenant lationship with our God and our brothers and sisters in Christ (anyi Chukwu na umu nne na umu nna n'ime Kristi gbara ndu). This venant relationship is rekindled every time we participate in Holy ass, and receive the Holy Body and Precious Blood of Christ to press this bond of reconciliation, communion, love and peace.

In the book of Ephesians 2:14-22, we read: "Christ has broken the lls of division between Greek and Jew, slave and free person, man d woman.... He is our peace.... has broken down the dividing wall

of enmity through His flesh…thus establishing peace and putti
enmity to death".

In this our Covenant in Christ, we have the Covenant m
(Eucharistia bu oriko anyi n'ime ogbugba ndu ohuru na Kristi). In t
Covenant meal (Oriko), we provide the bread and wine (achicha
mmanya), and Christ gives (provides) the Eucharist. And as each
us participates in the Eucharist, the expressions of our hearts rema
I come clean of anything against any member of Christ's body (
leenu aka/obi/mmuo m ooh, elu na ala leenu aka/obo/mmuo m o
aka/obi/mmuo m dikwa ocha ooh (ihe onye metere oburu ooh).

Friend, do you now understand why the Word of God admonis
us Cor 11:27-39? "Therefore, whoever eats the bread and drinks
cup of the Lord unworthily will have to answer for the body and blo
of the Lord…. That is why many among you are ill and infirm, an
considerable number are dying". Friend, do you now see why th
should be no enmity (Iro), no hostility (Ibu agha), no bitterness (C
ilu), no acrimony (ndokasi ahu), no resentment (ikpo asi), no er
and jealousy (Anya ufu) and no damaging gossips among brothers a
sisters in Christ? And do you now see, friend, why God admonishes
in his Word? "Owe one another nothing except mutual love" (Rom
3:8).

Indeed, the Eucharist is community-building, and ought to bu
faith communities into communities of love.

Friend, remember always Psalm 26: God is the vindicator
the just; Psalm 52: God punishes evil deeds; and Psalm 76: Go
deliverance awaits the innocent.

Friend, each time you want to attend Holy Mass, read this Bi
text of the letter to the Hebrews 12:22-24 at home before setting
to the Church:

> You have approached mount Zion,
>
> and the city of the living God
>
> and the heavenly Jerusalem,
>
> and countless angels in festival gathering,
>
> and the assembly of the firstborn enrolled in heaven,

and God the judge of all,

and the spirits of the just made perfect,

and Jesus, the mediator of the new covenant

and the sprinkled blood that speaks more eloquently than the blood of Abel

Friend, let us conclude this sermon by singing the Eucharistic mn again: *N'oriri Di Aso....* Amen!

71.   John 6:1-69

"Eat My Flesh, Drink My Blood"

Some Aspects of the Spirituality of Holy Mass

Friend, before we begin to look at the Spirituality of the H
Mass from the vantage point of this long discourse by Jesus on "eat
his body and drinking his blood" as recorded sorely in the Gos
according to St. John, we cannot allow to slip by the introduct
dialogue to this discourse. The crowd asks Jesus: "Rabbi, when
you get here?" (John 6:25). And Jesus retorted: I know why you
looking for me (cf. John 6:26).

Today, Jesus addresses this same question to you and to me: W
are you looking for me? The primary reason why each person sho
be looking for Jesus in his or her life should be to know God, l
him, worship him in this life, and to attain the blessed Christian h
to be with God forever in heaven. If there is any other reason you
looking for God, that becomes secondary.

For Catholics, the context for the realization of the "Will" of Je
Christ to give us his body to eat and his blood to drink is the H
Mass.

Friend, I want to reflect with you on some aspects of the Spiritua
of Holy Mass.

At Holy Mass, we express in a most profound manner one of
cardinal tenets of Catholic faith: "I believe in the Communion
Saints". Some people have always asked me these questions: Why
priests still say at the beginning of Consecration "Pray my broth
and Sisters…" and again, "…and you my brothers and sisters" at
Confiteor even when they are celebrating Holy Mass alone? Why
you bless empty pews and empty spaces at Holy Mass and benedict
and not limit the blessing to areas where there are people?

Friend, know this, that even if I am celebrating the Holy Mass alo
I will still do the same. When we express our belief in the Commun
of Saints, we are referring to the whole Church triumphant, milit

d purifying. These three arms of the one Church are present at
ch Holy Mass. Attendance at holy Mass, therefore, is not limited
us who form the immediate visible assembly, but also includes the
stant visible assembly (those of us who were not able to make it to
oly Mass and the invisible assembly of the Church in Heaven and
e Church in Purgatory. Something greater than the Altar and a
ngregation greater than us is present at Holy Mass (Cf. Matt 12:6).

Holy Mass, therefore, the celebration of the Body and Blood of
irist, we express this "Spiritual Communion of all Believers" in a
ost profound manner. This spiritual communion makes it possible,
I stand here celebrating as a priest, for the Pope also to stand with
e, all the Bishops and priests of the World stand with me, all believers
e around me.

Friend, this is why the blessing of the Holy mass, and indeed each
oly Mass celebrated goes beyond the immediate visible assembly,
d reaches out to even your people at home, to all Christians, and
deed, to the entire world. And this is why each morning, as I get up
om sleep and offer God my "virgin worship" and intentions for the
w day, my first prayer to God is:

"Lord God, as I thank you for my life and for this new day, I unite
self, my intentions and my entire family to the sacrifice of our Lord
us Christ on the altar of Calvary present on the altar of Holy Mass
is day in the Church throughout the world. I also unite myself, my
entions and my entire family to the Psalms of oblation, worship and
anksgiving being offered to God this day in the Church throughout
e world. And I unite myself, my intentions and my entire family to
e Holy Beads of the Most Holy Rosary of the Immaculate Virgin
ary through her intercession, asking that I and my entire family be
vered in the holy mantle of her motherly protection forever. Amen!"

Friend, be spiritually connected. The Holy Mass, the context of
lization of the Holy Body and Precious Blood, is indeed a "Spiritual
ommunion" of all believers, in which and through which the whole
ation, through us, gives worship to the Most Holy Trinity, and
rough which God's blessings continually flows out to believers
d entire creation, and in it, the Sacrament of the Holy Body and
ecious Blood of Christ is made available to all. This is why in the
charistic Prayer 3, we pray: "You are indeed Holy, oh Lord, and all

creation rightly gives you praise…you never cease to gather a peo to yourself so that from the East to the West, a pure sacrifice may offered to your name".

Friend, let us keep this spiritual communion alive, active a fruitful through our worthy participation. Let us always by faith beyond the natural and ordinary to perceive the extraordinary a supernatural things that God is doing at Holy Mass and among us.

Friend, remember: we cannot encounter God and rem unchanged.

Let us conclude this reflection with this hymn:

Holy Ghost, Do it again, do it again in my life today. Open eyes, to see Jesus, seated upon the Throne. Amen!

1Kings 19:1-9; John 6:1-69

"Body of Christ" and "Body and Blood of Christ"

Friend, we are still on the very rich theological discourse of Jesus the Gospel of John Chapter 6. I have already reflected on the Eucharist as Covenant, as well as on some aspects of the Spirituality Holy Mass. Let us as well reflect on the resulting controversy with the Galileans. After what seems a long and boring teaching, Jesus hits the nail on the head: "The Bread that I will give is my flesh for the life of the world" (John 6:51). Earlier he says: "I am the living bread that came down from heaven. Whoever eats this bread will live forever".

Friend, we must, here, make a distinction between the "Mystical Body of Christ" which is the Church, and the "Body and Blood of Christ" which is the Eucharist. The last is the subject of discourse of Jesus in John 6:1-51. In this discourse, Jesus goes beyond "Word became Flesh" (John 1:14) to talk of his flesh becoming "bread and drink".

The problem of the Galileans in this "body and blood" controversy is that the reality before them was different from their expectation: how can he be the bread from Heaven just like that? I want you to recall what they said in John 7:27: "Yet we know where this man is from; but when the Messiah comes, no one will know where he is from". Thunder, lightning, burning bush, chariots of fire – these are the extraordinary things the Galileans are familiar with. And that is why they are unable to see God when he works in ordinary ways.

However, borrowing the words the Angel speaks to Prophet Elijah in 1Kings 19:7-9" "'Get up and eat, else the journey will be too long'....He got up, ate and drank; then, strengthened by that food, he walked forty days and forty nights to the mount of God, Horeb", Jesus impresses on them that if we believe and eat his body and drink his blood in the Eucharist, we will be alive and we will reach heaven when he says: "I am the living bread that came down from heaven, whoever eats this bread will live forever" (John 6:51).

Friend, the Eucharist is indeed the pledge of life and immortality for all who believe. In this regard, it is important that 1Corinthians

(Chapters 11 and 10) calls for purity of heart. I say: "Blessed are t
clean of heart, they shall encounter Christ in the Eucharist". T
Question is not whether Christ comes to us or not in the Euchari
the question is whether we are able to recognize him. And that is w
the statement of Jesus in this discourse is instructive: "No one com
to me unless the father who sent me draws him" (John 6:45). In tl
statement, Jesus reminds us that faith is a gift.

Friend, you don't leave the Church, or abandon the Eucharist,
disown some articles of faith just because you do not understand. St
on! Let us, in humility, ask God to teach us, to open our eyes, to op
our hearts, to open our minds, and fill them with the light of Fai
Amen!

Isaiah 6:1-2a, 3-8; I Cor 15:1-11; Luke 5:1-11

Fear is like Cholesterol

Before the all-holy, all-good and all-true God, Isaiah exclaims: "Woe me I am doomed, for I am a man of unclean lips" (Isaiah 6:5a); Apostle ul exclaims: "I am not fit to be called an apostle" (ICor15:9); and ostle Peter exclaims: "Depart from me, Lord, for I am a sinful man" ike 5:8).

Friend, the more, indeed, we encounter our all-good, all-holy and -true God, the more, indeed, we discover how sinful we mortals are. is is because we all are naked before God (Anyi nile gba oto n'ihu ukwu).

The discovery of our sinfulness before God leads us to fear. Fear is like olesterol: there is the bad cholesterol (LDL) and the good cholesterol DL), There is bad fear that can lead to paralysis before God, and there good fear (reverential fear) that builds up in us confidence in God. re, we are talking about good fear.

Because of this discovery of our own sinfulness before God, there ould be no room in us for a feeling or showing of self-righteousness, lier-than-thou attitude or unnecessary spiritual arrogance.

Jesus tell his Apostles as he tell us: "Put out into the deep water and ver your nets for a catch" (). We see, here, that when we sincerely offer our weaknesses and limitations to Jesus, he is able to bring forth best ults out of these weaknesses and limitations. It is God who brings v the proud and raises the lowly. There should be no room in us any form of spiritual arrogance, "for in the stomach of each of us found feces". We must always endeavor to be spiritually humble. In ing charity, think more of others and less of yourself. But in seeking d pursuing spiritual growth and maturity, be consistent: think less of ers and more of yourself.

Friend, may the spiritual humility of Isaiah, Paul and Peter, and the ength that Jesus offers become also your humility and your strength your spiritual pilgrimage to God and in your ardent desire to make ven. Amen!

74.   Genesis 9:8-15; I Peter 3:18-22; Mark 1:12-15

Jesus in the Wilderness: A Replica of our Individual Experiences

Friend, every Ash Wednesday in Lent, we have ashes imposed on o foreheads. The Ashes remind us of:

- Our humility before God as mere mortals who must, one d come to the end of our earthly lives• Our sinfulness, and c repentance thereof•   Our pilgrimage as persons on their w to our true home in Heaven, that other life which does not co to an end but lasts forever.

Lent becomes a time when God draws us nearer to Him, and wh we renew our relationship and friendship with God. Lent is more abo God's love for us and our love of God than about sin and Hell. Le is motivated by this love than the dread for Satan and the fear of H What we do during the holy season of lent is to renew this relationsh of love through our Lenten discipline: intensify our spiritual appetite prayer, word of God, abstinence, almsgiving, acts of penance and oth acts of devotion such as the Stations of the Cross.

In the Gospel periscope, according to St. Mark, describing the des experience of Jesus, we read: "The Spirit immediately drove him out i the wilderness. He was in the wilderness forty days, tempted by Sat and he was with the wild beasts, and the angels waited on him" (M 1:12-13).

Friend, in this wilderness of Jesus' temptation, we observe presence of the Spirit of God, Angels, Satan, and wild beasts. There is a the unmentioned: the spiritual and physical need of Jesus This Scriptu picture or language is a replica of my world and your world in which have found ourselves: In this world, as we grapple with our spiritual a material needs, the Holy Spirit and the Angels of God are at work, Satan and his wild beasts (demons) are also at work.

Friend, in this individual wilderness experience, while the Spirit God and the Angels of God are all around to draw us towards God a give us spiritual strength, Satan and his demons would try hard to p down and away from God into an abyss of insincerity, vainglory and ritual weakness. This struggle continues through life; and sometimes cooperating with grace we triumph, and sometimes by negligence we are overwhelmed into sin.

The text from Apostle Peter talks of our baptism in Christ. This is so prefigured in the text from Genesis where Noah and his household were saved by God through "baptism" in the waters of the Deluge.

As Lent is a special time of Retreat for the whole Church in proximate preparation for Easter when we renew our baptismal vows to God, may the grace of Lent purify our consciences, give us the spiritual strength to stand for God and withstand Satan, and renew our commitment to the Church, to our families and to society. May the Holy Spirit of God and the Holy Angels continue to help us in our sincere struggles to overcome Satan and his wild beasts (Demons) in the wilderness of life until we get to our true homeland in heaven. Amen!

75.   Acts 1:1-11; Eph 1:17-23; Matt 28:16-20

Overwhelmed by Christ's Fidelity to His Church

Friend, at every feast of the Ascension of the Lord, we are faced with the eternal truth that Christ Jesus is gone for a while, but that he will back!

Before he left to his father, he said the His Church: "I will not leave you as orphans; I will be with you. Before long, the world will not see anymore, but you will see me…. Because I live…" (John 14:18-19). also made this promise to her: "And I tell you, you are Peter, and on t rock I will build my church, and the gates of hell shall not prevail agai it" (Matt 16:18).

Friend, whenever I reflect on how Christ Jesus has been faithful his promises, and accompanied the Church through the ages with gr men and women of heroic sanctity, courage and wisdom who emerge periods of great need in the Church, I am overwhelmed by God's fide to his promises. See how, in our time, Christ has blessed his Church w men and women of heroic sanctity, courage and great wisdom as Bless John Paul II, Blessed Mother Theresa, Pope Benedict XVI (Emerit and Pope Francis. And Christ will not abandon his Church, today in c time nor in the future, as the gates of Hades shall never prevail agai the Holy Church of Christ.

May the Holy Spirit continue to help the Church in her univer local and particular levels to feel more of Christ's abiding presen Amen!

5.   Matt 25:14-30; Matt 6:19-24; Mark 11:23

To whom much is Given, Much will be Expected

Friend, "to whom much is given, much will be expected" is a statement made by Jesus in the Gospel according to Luke (Luke 12:48). This statement simply calls us to gratitude to God and to responsibility whatever we receive from him: If we are blessed with grace, talents, wealth, knowledge, time, and the like, it is expected that we use these well to glorify God and benefit others. That is why people who were great sinners worked like bulls and ran like wounded lions in the race faith. Apostle Paul, Disciple Mary Magdalene, St. Augustine: They displayed handsome good will to God and burning desire for the things God. And this is what the ungrateful servant in Matthew 25:14-30, who dug in the ground to hide his master's money, lacked. The problem this servant was not that he could not make some effort. His problem was bad will and ingratitude. God has shown each of us lots of gratitude. How do we translate these into fortunes for the Church as we recall our spiritual and material treasures as Christians? Let us remember, here, the words of Jesus in Matt 6:19-24:

"Do not lay up for yourselves treasures on earth, where moth and rust destroy and where thieves break in and steal, but lay up for yourselves treasures in heaven, where neither moth nor rust destroy and where thieves do not break in and steal. For where your treasure is, there your heart will be, also. The eye is the lamp of the body. So, if your eye is healthy, your whole body will be full of light, but if your eye is bad, your whole body will be full of darkness. If then the light in you is darkness, how great is the darkness! No one can serve two masters, for either he will hate the one and love the other, or he will be devoted to the one and despise the other. You cannot serve God and money".

The Church is being repeatedly forced through persecution by enemies of religion who capitalize on the moral weaknesses of her members, and through legislations by nationalities and world organs, give up values that she has treasured through the centuries. Even, some Church communities have sold their patrimony in order to remain afloat. Family and family values are under attacks and in some places. Christians can no longer publicly exercise their faith and beliefs. Here,

St. Lawrence the deacon becomes a handy example of one who, in gratitu
to God for unmerited blessings, accepted martyrdom in 258 AD protecti
the treasures of the Church of Rome in his custody rather than hand the
over to Pagan Emperor Valerian after the marytrodm of Pope Sixtus II a
four Deacon assistants..

Friend, do you remember what Pope Benedict XVI (emeritus) sa
some time ago: that today, a worse persecution of the Church is fro
within, from inside, from her own children who live lives of scandal th
weaken the Gospel. In the face of attacks to decimate the spiritual a
material treasure of the Church, we are called to intense prayer, a mo
intense commitment to our Christian life and steadfastness in defendi
publicly the tenets of our faith and the values we hold sacred even wh
this entails martyrdom.

Friend, the shortest distance is that from the head to the hea
But many rarely cover it in a lifetime. We often prefer to rema
predominantly persons of the head than the heart. Could this be a
result of hearts made infertile and unattractive either by personal choi
society or environment, or that people do not see why they should
to the trouble? Again, in-between the head and the heart is the mou
Indeed, Christian discipleship requires all those whose heads are sob
whose hearts are healthy as the anchor points, and whose mouths se
the tranquility of the duo. For any society that is bereft of soul, a lit
candle lighted and shinning in one dark corner can surely reduce t
darkness. Friend, you might be that candle. You and I might be t
instruments of positive change that human society so much needs tod

Friend, in the Gospel according to Mark (11:23), the faith to mo
a mountain does not indicate that the deed is done by us: it is still G
who does it, and in his own time, and in his own way. This faith alwa
entails, therefore, that we be patient for him to do it, and confident th
he will surely do something.

May we, through the intercession of St. Lawrence Deacon, contir
to display gratitude to God, continue to store our treasure in heaven, a
do all with patient and confident faith. Amen!

7.   Ezekiel 28:1-12; Matthew 19:16-33; 23:1-12

Possessions and Authority (Power)

In the Gospel according to Luke, Jesus says: "Suppose one of you wants to build a tower. Will he not first sit down and estimate the cost to see if he has enough money to complete it? For if he lays the foundation and is not able to finish it, everyone who sees it will ridicule him, saying, 'his fellow began to build and was not able to finish...' In the same way, any of you who does not give up everything he has cannot be my disciple. Salt is good, but if it loses its saltiness, how can it be made salty again? It is fit neither for the soil nor for the manure pile; it is thrown out. He who has ears to hear let him hear." (Luke 14:28-30, 33-35)

Friend, it is against the background of the above quotation that we can appraise the questions of the young man, the response of Jesus, the reaction of the young man, and the rebuff of Jesus in Matthew 19:16-33. Is this young man actually ready for the consequences of his seemingly sincere and innocent inquiry?

The response of Jesus is this simple message: Young man, to gain eternal life, you have two things to offer the world: religion and material wellbeing. This has consequence for both the Church and individual Christians. The Church as *Sacramentum Mundi* extends her charitable services to the suffering humanity and suffering nature. This is why the Church assists to better the conditions through which men and women come seeking God. The Church, therefore, participates in the historical processes that promote respect for life and integrity of creation. This is also why each Christian must always participate in this same process.

Friend, note, therefore, that in the second part of this Matthew 19:16-, Jesus' rebuff is not a condemnation of possession or wealth *in se* but a condemnation of attitude. Jesus could not have condemned possessions since they can be blessings to us from God. He teaches that the proper attitude is to see possessions not as ends in themselves, but as a means. And the end is the glory of God and wellbeing of all. Christ warns us of attitude of "haughtiness of heart" (also echoed in the above text from prophet Ezekiel), often leading one to displace God with self-ego-I, and greed, which excludes others from sharing in our blessings. Jesus asks

for humility of heart putting God at the center of our lives, life eve
and possessions.

Friend, because of the necessary connection between possessi
wealth and authority/power, Jesus again teaches in the Gospel passage
Matthew 23:1-12 that our attitude to positions and authority must a
change. Jesus is generally harsh to those in positions of authority a
who wield power as he was to the Scribes and Pharisees. This is beca
positions, authority, power, are not ends in themselves; they are a me
to an end; and the end is responsibility and service; otherwise they
become monstrous. When position, authority, power becomes an e
there is abuse of office, and people suffer; but when position, author
power is seen as a means to service, people are enhanced, and the gi
of all gifts, God, is glorified.

The CCC asserts: "It remains for the holy people to struggle, w
grace from on high, to obtain the good things God promises. In or
to possess and contemplate God, Christ's faithful mortify their cravi
and, with the grace of God, prevail over the seductions of pleasure a
power".

May all who find themselves in positions of wealth, authority a
power, in the family, in the church, and in the civil society, dispense a
exercise them according to God's mind and wellbeing of all. Amen.

Gen 3:9-15, 20; Eph 1:3-6, 11-12; Luke 1:26-38

We Share in Her Immaculateness

Friend, the dogma of the Immaculate Conception defined by Pope
us IX on December 8, 1854, with the Papal Bull *"Ineffabilis Deus"*
(fallible God) states:

"The Most Blessed Virgin Mary, from the first moment of her
nception, by a singular grace and privilege of Almighty God, and by
tue of the merits of Jesus Christ, the savior of the human race, was
eserved immune from all stain of original sin" (CCC n. 504).

This means that the Blessed Virgin Mary was born immaculate and
nained immaculate all her life in view of her predestined role as mother
the Savior. The logical extension of this privilege is the Assumption of
e Blessed Virgin Mary's body and soul into Heaven, and her coronation
Queen Mother of Heaven and Earth. Of all creatures of God, only the
essed Virgin Mary shares in this unique privilege.

But friend, all of her children by adoption in Christ Jesus participate
her privilege through our baptisms. When we were baptized, we were
ade to participate in her unique privilege: we were made immaculate
rough the wiping out of original sin in the waters of Christian
generation.

However, the ancient dragon mentioned in the Book of Revelation
ev 12:1-6), whose head the Woman and Her Son crushes, and who
s unable to disfigure her Immaculateness, is now a ravaging wolf at
r with all of Her adopted children to lure them to offend God and
secrate their "participated baptismal immaculateness". Jesus Christ
ticipated this and has bequeathed to the Church the Sacrament of
conciliation. Even though we can often fall into sin, each time we
cerely approach God in the confessional, God restores our baptismal
nocence; our "participated baptismal immaculateness" is restored,
newed by the same merit of Jesus Christ, the only Savior of the World.

Having been exalted above the Angels and Saints and now at the
ht hand of her only son, Jesus Christ our Lord, dressed in Gold of
phir (Cf. Psalm 45:9b), with a crown of twelve stars on her head, and

the moon as her footstool (Rev 12:1), she presents us and our petitie in a most efficacious manner to her Son in Heaven. What she asks obtains, and her pleas can never be unheard.

Friend, let us not forget to pray: "Hail Mary, Full of Grace, the Le is with you (Luke 1:28). Blessed art thou amongst women; And bles. is the fruit of thy womb, Jesus (Luke 1:42). Holy Mary, Mother of G (Luke 1:35b). Pray for us sinners now, and at the hour of our dea Amen!

We pray that through the powerful intercession of the Blessed Vir Mary, the Queen Mother of Heaven and Earth, we may continue to obedient to God's Will, faithful to our baptismal vows, and loyal to Church of her son, Jesus Christ. Amen.

. Isaiah 55:1-2; Philippians 2:1-11; Matt 14:13-21

Conviviality (Uto-Nwanne)

In the Scripture text from Prophet Isaiah, God invites all of his venanted children to come and enjoy His blessings without pay. Note, *initio*, that "without pay" does not mean "without cost".

Friend, if God were to charge you money for all his favors to you including your life), how much do you think you would pay?

However, in the Gospel text from Apostle Matthew, Jesus tells us at we don't have to pay anything; the only cost, the only expectation us, is for us to continue to share what we have with one another in atmosphere of conviviality (Uto-Nwanne). And Jesus demonstrates werfully that if we are able to share God's blessings with one another, will always have more than enough.

Friend, consider a family, a community, a society, a world where ery person is ready to share what he or she has with others, what a perabundance there will be. The Eucharist we celebrate and share plicates this superabundance, this conviviality for us.

Hence, in the scripture text from Philippians, Apostle Paul reminds of the love of God made available and accessible in Jesus Christ: rist's self-donation and immolation for our salvation is *motif* for our ing good and kind to one another.

May God, through the Eucharistic communion, continue to move r hearts to gratitude that is expressed in loving sharing and conviviality. nen!

80. Wisdom 6: 12-16; 1Thess 4:13-18; Matt 25:1-13

Prudence and Preparedness versus Presumption and Negligen

Friend, we are all very familiar with the Parable of the Ten Virgins in Gospel according to Apostle Matthew. Let me, in this sermon, dramatiz for us to get to the full import of the message. These Ten Virgins are invi to the banquet of Eternal Life. In the process of their preparation, t argument ensued:

Five Wise Virgins: As we prepare to go to this wedding, let us take ex oil for our lamps!

Five Foolish Virgins: (Sigh) Don't bother yourselves; the program is and everything will work out according to schedule! We'll sort things ou

Five Wise Virgins: What if the groom arrives late?

Five Foolish Virgins: Why are you girls always pessimistic? Let's go t (please); just hope for the best!

Five Wise Virgins: Well, as for us, we're taking extra oil, oh!

Friend, you know the rest of the story.

The Scripture text from the prophetic book of Wisdom says: "For tak thought of wisdom is the perfection of prudence, and whoever for her s keeps vigil shall quickly be free of care" (Wisdom 6:16).

Friend, wisdom is also about taking the right decisions and mak the right choices in life. Some people run into the danger of hoping for best out of life without preparing for the worst. Prudence and preparedn here, comes face to face with presumption and negligence. Which way you go, friend?

In ultimate prudence and preparedness, Apostle Paul in 1Thess 4:13 admonishes that, as covenanted children of God in Christ Jesus, we mus all wisdom always prepare for our end (going back to God) since all mor must die. This call to prepare to die must be heeded in all prudence, with however being hunted by the predictions of the so-called "end of time" fa prophets who think that they have privileged access to God's timetable.

May we not be found wanting when Jesus comes. Amen!

. Acts 3:6-8 & 4:10; John 21:1-14; Luke 24:32; Matt
:51-54

ast your Net for a Catch: the Name, the Word, the Blood

Friend, in the healing of the cripple in Acts of the Apostle, Peter says:
have neither silver nor gold but what I do have, I give you: in the name
Jesus Christ the Nazarene, rise and walk" (Acts 3:6); and Peter affirms:
his man stands before you healed in the name of Jesus" (Acts 4:10).

What does this tell us? – There is power in the Name of Jesus!

At the Lake of Tiberias, Jesus orders his followers: "Friends, cast your
t over the right side for a catch" (John 21:6). And they obeyed. Again,
: hearts of Cleopas and the other disciple burn within them (they are
on fire) as Jesus speaks the scriptures to them (Cf. Luke 24:32).

What does this tell us? There is power in the Word of God! (Cf. also
n 4:48-54).

During the crucifixion, one of the soldiers pierces Jesus' side with
ance and, when His Blood and Water poured out on the soil of
usalem: "At that moment the curtain of the temple was torn in two
m top to bottom. The earth shook, the rocks split and the tombs broke
en. The bodies of many holy people who had died were raised to life.
ey came out of the tombs after Jesus' resurrection and went into the
ly city and appeared to many people. When the centurion and those
th him who were guarding Jesus saw the earthquake and all that had
ppened, they were terrified, and exclaimed, 'Surely he was the Son of
d!'" (Matt 27:51-54). Again, after the resurrection of Jesus, "while he
s with them at table, he took bread, said the blessing, broke it, and
e it to them. With that, their eyes were opened and they recognized
n" (Luke 24:30-31).

What does this tell us? There is power in the Holy Body and precious
od of Jesus!

Friend, do you now understand what happens when, in faith, blessing,
aling and deliverance are pronounced upon you **"in the Name of
us Christ, by the power of His Blood, and in the authority of his
rd"**? This becomes even more efficacious since Heavenly powers

(much more potent than any other power) have been made availa
to us though the death and resurrection of Jesus Christ. As Apo
Peter tells us in Acts 2:21, "everyone who calls on the name of the L
will be saved". Whenever we call on the name of Jesus Christ in Pra
spiritual energies are released to us and into us because there is po
in his name; whenever we listen to the word of God, spiritual ener
are released to us and into us, because in the Scriptures, Jesus Ch
speaks to us directly and his words come with power; and whene
we receive the Holy Body and Precious Blood of Jesus Christ, spirit
energies are released to us and into us because we become one with h
for "Whoever eats my flesh and drinks my blood remains in me, an
in him" (John 6:56).

But let's take the Lake Tiberias encounter further:

The Apostles going fishing (John 21:3): Peter announces to the ot
Apostles – "I am going fishing". And they replied, "We will also go w
you".

What does this tell us? Often there is the temptation for us to
more on what we can do ourselves and less *on what God can do with*

Christ's Appearance and Actions (John 21:4-5): "At dawn, Jesus
standing on the shore...asking them, "Have you caught anything?"

What does this tell us? Yes, we can think about and act well
ourselves sometimes, but God thinks about and acts best for
perpetually. Remember the Hymn: "Ihe ahu nakpa m n'emetu Gi nna

Friend, to conclude, these incidents clearly demonstrate to us
truth of the words of the Gospel in Matthew 6:33: "But seek ye first
kingdom, and his righteousness; and all these things shall be added u
you". "Jesus is the same yesterday, today and forever" (Hebrew 13:8).
lives, in his name, in his word, and he is present in the Eucharist.

May the prophesy in these hymns continue to enrich us with blessir
Ihe ahu n'akpa m; Obu n'aha Jesus ka mmadu nile gbakore n'ebea; Ok
ya bu eee na eeemen; obu ya, obu ya, obu ya nwaturu Chukwu. Ame

. **Malachi 3:19-20a; 2Thess 5:1-6; Luke 21:5-19**

Doomsday!

Friend, each year as we approach the end of the Church's liturgical [yea]r, the liturgical readings, especially the Gospels, concentrate on the [ter]rible and scary pictures of events that will signal the approach of the [en]d of the world. These scary events are about the end of evil and the [fin]al decimation of Satan. That is why at the end of each of those scary [pass]ages, God pronounces encouraging words: "Remain faithful until [de]ath, and I will give you the crown of life" (Rev 20:10c); "Not a hair [of] your head will be destroyed. By your perseverance, you will secure [yo]ur lives" (Luke 21:18-19); "Stand erect and raise your heads because [yo]ur redemption is at hand" (Luke 21;28). So, at the end of it all, God's [me]ssage to his children is: My children, do not be afraid (Umu Chukwu, [un]u atula egwu).

Friend, let us not, therefore, succumb to the dread of the ultimate [ev]ents. Let us, rather, hold on to the encouraging and reassuring words [fro]m God as we sing *"marana tha"* – Come, Lord Jesus: Come and end [evi]l in the world and give victory to your faithful children.

In the reading from Prophet Jeremiah, God speaks of raising up a new [sho]ot. I want you to imagine a new shoot sprouting up from a withered [bra]nch: it is all about preparation, renewal and interior decoration of our [liv]es; it is about God doing something new in our lives.

Friend, every day, as we remain vigilant, waiting for the return of [th]e Lord, let us continue to sing with the psalmist: "Lord, let me know [yo]ur ways, teach me your paths, guide me to your truth" (Psalm 25:4-5). [Am]en!

83.   John 3:1-6; Matt 3:13-17; Matt 28:16-20

My Baptism of New Creation in Grace

In John 3:1-6, Jesus tells Nicodemus: "I tell you the truth, no (
can enter the Kingdom of God unless he is born of water and the Spi
What is born of flesh is flesh, but what is born of Spirit is Spirit".

Friend, in this Gospel encounter of John 3:1-6, reference is made
baptism in Christ. Jesus alludes to the Sacrament of Christian initiat
which he will give and institute at the appropriate time.

In the Baptism of Jesus by John the Baptist (Matt 3:13-17; M
1:9-12; Luke 3:21-22; Cf. John 1:26, 32-34), beyond Christ's seemin
simplistic response to John "Let it be so now; for thus it is fitting fo
to fulfil all righteousness" (Matt 3:15)--Mee M ya, k'odi ka ana em
Jesus has an important teaching to do and a crucial message to give: "
presence of the Trinity (Father, Son and Holy Spirit), never heard in
baptism of John the Baptist, implies that at Baptism in Christ, a r
creation takes place. While John's baptism is the Baptism of repenta
for the forgiveness of Sins (Luke 3:3), Jesus' Baptism is baptism of N
Creation in Grace. In Christ, therefore, Christians enter into this r
creation through Christ's Sacrament of Christian Initiation.

It is in this light that we now understand and interpret the Mission
Mandate and Great Commission of Matthew 28:18-20: "All autho
in heaven and on earth has been given to me. Therefore, go and m
disciples of all nations, baptizing them in the name of the Father
of the Son and of the Holy Spirit, and teach them to obey everythir
have commanded you. Surely I am with you always, to the very enc
the age."

Friend, this is a categorical mandate and commission to the Chu
which is not race, color, gender nor age discriminatory. That is why
informative when we read from the Acts of the Apostles the Baptisr
practices of the first generation Christian Apostles and Disciples: A
10:1-48, Cornelius and all his household are baptized; Acts 16:11-
Lydia and all her household are baptized; Acts 15:25-34, the Philipp

ler and his entire family are baptized. In all of these cases, there is no stinction between adults and infants.

In the Catechism of the Catholic Church (CCC), the Church teaches that Baptism is important for salvation and eternal life because without ne birth of water and the Spirit", "no one can enter the kingdom of od" (Cf. CCC 1215): "Baptisma di mkpa maka nzoputa n'ihi ewetuo ptisma, onweghi onye puru iba n'eligwe".

Friend, no person has God's timetable for each person that He ings into this world. The Church, therefore, offers the opportunity : salvation and eternal life to old and young. After all, salvation and ernal life is given despite you or me. It is not given to you because you ve passed an exam or because your faculties have come to maturity d reason.

In the Christian calendar, we celebrate Lent with its dual strands: the nitential character and the baptismal character. Predominantly, the ripture readings in the third and fourth weeks of Lent bring out the age of water: Jesus meets the woman of Samaria at the Jacob's Well d promises "The Living Water" (John 4: 10); Jesus meets the crippled man who wishes to wash in the miraculous Pool of Bethesda, heals n and tells him not to sin anymore (Cf. John 5:7, 14); Prophet Ezekiel s a vision of water flowing forth from the Sanctuary in the temple ich "makes clean and gives life" (Ezekiel 47:1-9, 12). One principal ction of water is to clean persons and things. We become dirty after r daily jobs or after our sleep and we use water to clean up and to ell fresh again. These scripture texts read during Lent remind us of nt's penitential and baptismal significance, especially the spiritual ansing, the rebirth, the regeneration that Jesus through the Holy Spirit the Church offers us especially through the Sacraments of Christian itiation and reconciliation.

May the seed of grace sown into us through our baptism of new ation in Christ (Cf. Isaiah 65:17) or Christian regeneration continue grow us, like the biblical Mustard Seed, into "a chosen race, a royal iesthood, a holy nation, a people for [God's] own possession" (Preface f the Sunday in Ordinary time). Amen!

84. Exodus 17:3-7; Romans 5:1-2, 5-8; John 4:5-42

HUMAN THIRST!

Friend, we all are very much at home with the word. Thirst: We fee within us and we always hear ourselves say, "I'm thirsty". We always seek quench our thirst.

These three Scripture texts talk of Water flowing: The text from Exoc illustrates how Moses strikes the rock and water flows out. This incid is recorded to have taken place four months after the departure of Israelites from Egypt towards the Promised Land, Palestine. The text fr the Gospel according to Apostle John dramatizes how and where Jesu promising to give the living water which will not only satisfy every th but flow from within us to eternal life. The text from St. Paul's letter to Romans mentions that the love of God has been poured into our hea (like water) through the Holy Spirit.

Let us notice the link between the text from Exodus and that of Gospel: The incident of Exodus here is a prelude to the encounter betwe Jesus and the Samaritan Woman in the Gospel where Jesus would pron to give us living water. These readings underscore two thirsts that must satisfied in humans:

* The Physical thirst: that leads to mere physical satisfaction.

* The Spiritual thirst: that leads to profound spiritual satisfaction.

Jesus speaks of the water that he will give us. Our journey to this Je Well of the living water (not Jacob's well) where Jesus satisfies our spirit thirst and brings us spiritual satisfaction which begins with our baptisr waters.

Friend, Jesus' refreshing water in our souls makes us long to wors God and seek his face. If you've not come to a point in your life where thirst for God, the thirst for worshiping him, the thirst for the salvat of your soul, the thirst for heaven becomes a sweet experience (includ coming to Mass), where the thirst for living the Christian life becor something natural to you, then you need fresh flow of that living wa which only Jesus can give.

In other words, if worshipping God is still a burden to you rather than sweet experience, then you must take your yearly Renewal of Baptismal vows very seriously.

Remember too: Jesus is not only the Living Water; Jesus is also the bread of life, the Light of the World, the Good Shepherd, the Vine, the Resurrection and the Life, the Lamb of God. The more we thirst for and engage Jesus, the more he leads us into deeper and more committed relationship with him, the Holy Spirit and Father.

Friend, let us pray that the Eucharist (the sacrament of the Holy Body and Precious Blood of Christ) will continue to lead us to deepen that thirst for God which is above all other thirsts and help us give up whatever needs to be given up (our wrong ways of thinking, doing and talking) so that the Holy Spirit will continue to pour into our hearts like water, the love of God.

Let us note too, in the encounter between Jesus and the Samaritan woman, the progressive growth in this woman in her understanding of the person of Jesus: She first knows Jesus as "Sir"; she then recognizes and declares Jesus as "Prophet"; finally she confesses Jesus as "Messiah". As a result, she is transformed and she becomes an evangelizer for Jesus to the villagers. This same scenario involving knowledge, recognition, declaration, confession and transformation plays out also in the encounter between Jesus and the blind man in the Gospel according to St. John 9:1-41: The blind man first knows him as "the man called Jesus"; he, then, recognizes and declares Him as a "prophet; finally he confesses Him as "Lord". How have you progressed through your spiritual encounter with Jesus from mere knowledge about Him to recognition, declaration and confession of Him, and finally to your transformation unto discipleship? Are you growing in this spiritual encounter? How has your deeper understanding of who Jesus Christ is transformed you into active imitator of Christ participant in his mission (Cf. I Corinthians 11:1).

As Moses struck the Rock and water flowed out, so may Christ continue to strike our hearts so that the love of God poured into our hearts at baptism may continue to transform us and turn us into evangelizers for God. Amen!

85. Acts 1:7-9, 12-14; John 14:5-6; Genesis 3:14-15; Luke 1:28, 42

"No One comes to the Father Except through Me"

The Place of the Immaculate Virgin Mary in Salvation

- Mary, Mother of Jesus participated in the first ever *Life in Spirit* seminar leading up to the Pentecost. Why wouldn't she Mary, Mother of Jesus not the Spouse of the Holy Spirit?

"No one comes to the Father except through me."

Friend, the Blessed Virgin Mary, mother of Christ, is an act participant in the life and passion of her son. The Mother of God is a there actively present in the first ever held "life in the Spirit semin leading up to the Pentecost.

Some mainline protestant churches and Pentecostals have always course out of ignorance) criticized the Catholic Church for her devot to the Blessed Virgin Mother of God. They have denounced the Ros of the Blessed Virgin Mary, and even go as far as casting aspersions the Mother of Christ. One often hear these misinformed brothers a sisters ask: "Why do you pray to Mary? Why do you pray to the sair Why can't you pray to God directly? After all, Jesus said that no comes to the father except through me!"

Friend, I want to ask you: Don't Catholics go to God through Chr Don't you hear our prayers end with "Through Christ our Lord..." Christ no longer the head of the Church? (Colossians 1:18)?

Friend, the *proto-evangelium* of Genesis 3:14-15 presents the won and her offspring as principal figures in the war against Satan. And points to the Immaculate Virgin and her son, Jesus Christ. Mary is given the special privilege of being the Mother of God just to bear Je in her womb, deliver Jesus to the world, and then be trashed. No! role is to deliver Jesus to us and to point us to Jesus. Look at the ev of the Wedding feast at Cana in Galilee where Mary sends the pec to Jesus: "Do what he tells you" (Cf. John 2:1-12). Look at the even the visitation of Mary to Elizabeth where after the greeting and eul

Elizabeth, Mary points Elizabeth to God by exclaiming; "My soul rifies the Lord…" (Luke 1:46-55).

Friend, the Rosary is biblical; it is embedded in the Sacred Scriptures m beginning to end and including all the Mysteries of the Rosary yful, luminous, sorrowful and glorious). In the Catholic Church we not orphans: we have father and we have mother. If we sinners can ty, intercede and supplicate for one another, saints of God in Heaven 1 do that for me too, and do it even better.

Friend, both Susanna (Daniel 10) and the adulterous woman (John -11) would have been dead except for the grace of God…. We would ve all been dead (spiritually and physically) except for the grace of God. e three old men of Daniel 10 always reminds me of Proverbs 6:16-19, ting, three things (among others) that God abhors: A poor person o is haughty, an old person who is a liar, and an educated person o lacks common sense. Many Christians today have over-trusted ir poor knowledge, many have ignorantly lied against the Holy Spirit; d many a learned Christian have exhibited an embarrassing lack of nmon sense in the things of God, forgetting that we believe, proclaim d celebrate in the Church God's wisdom over human wisdom.

Let us pray:

Hail Mary, full of grace.

The Lord is with thee.

Blessed art thou among women,

and blessed is the fruit of thy womb, Jesus.

Holy Mary, Mother of God,

pray for us sinners,

now and at the hour of our death.

Amen!

Devotional Hymn to BVM:

Ekele Maria, Nne nke Chukwu…Anyi edo gi mmamma

Ekele Maria, Nne ndi otu Kristi…

Ekele Maria, Nne di ocha…

Ekele Maria, Nne di itunanya…

Ikele Maria, Igbe Ogbugbandu…

Ekele Maria, Kpakpandu Ututu…

Ekele Maria, Nkasi obi ndi no n'afufu…

Ekele Maria, Ezenwanyi nke udo…

Ekele Maria, Onye ogbugbo ndi njo…

Ekele Maria, Ahu ike ndi oria…

Ekele Maria, Nne ezi-na-ulo…

Ekene Maria, Nne huru umu ya n'anya…

Ekene Maria, egwu ekwensu…

Anyi eto gi mmamma… anyi eto gi mmamma (20times)

Nwaturu nke Chukwu, Onye n'ekpochapu njo nke uwa,

Mere anyi oh ebere (twice)

Nwaturu nke Chukwu, Onye n'ekpochapu njo nke uwa,

Mere anyi oh, mere anyi oh, mere anyi oh ebere!

. Isaiah 22:19-23; Romans 9:3-5; Matthew 16:13-20

Servant-Leaders in the Church

Friend, in the passage of the Gospel according to blessed Apostle atthew, Our Lord Jesus Christ appoints blessed Apostle Peter the ad of the Church. This passage, when read alongside John 21:15-17 ere our Lord Jesus Christ tell Apostle Peter to "feed my lambs… d my sheep", makes the strong point that after Jesus Christ, the Holy ther (Pope) is the chief shepherd, head of the Church, and visible resentative of Christ.

However, our Lord Jesus Christ has not left Peter to do all the work ne. He gives Peter helpers: we remember here the college of apostles att 10:1-15) and the appointment of the Seventy-two (Luke 10:1-12).

In Ex 18:21, Moses is advised, "…look among all the people for able d God fearing men, trustworthy men who hate dishonest gain, and them as officers over groups of thousands, of hundreds, of fifties, and tens". And in Acts 6:3-4, the Apostles instruct, "Brothers, select from ong you seven reputable men, filled with the Holy Spirit and wisdom om we shall appoint to this task, whereas we shall devote ourselves to yer and to the ministry of the word".

Nonetheless, in the Scripture text of Isaiah 22:19-23, we read of ebna who occupies the most powerful position in the kingdom of King zekiah of Judah. But in this Scripture passage, God relieves Shebna of t position and places Eliakim in that position.

Friend, this is a reminder to us by God that we are God's servants; re is time for everything under the sun (and especially in the Church), re is a time to assume a particular responsibility for God and a time vacate office. Take and hold does not mean take for keeps (*nara jiji ughi nara were*). There comes a time when God anoints people for a tain office (especially in the Church) and there comes a time when He ieves people of office and places those he chooses in those positions. the Church, we are not Kings and subjects (**Oha-na-eze**), we are God's usehold at worship (**Oha-ofufe Chukwu**) (Cf. Romans 9:3-5). And en it comes to choosing servant-leaders (especially in the Church), d is the sponsor and the Holy Spirit is the kingmaker. In the mission

of the Church God has his way of providing round pegs in round hc
and square pegs in square holes. When God makes you a servant-lea
in the church, he gives you all the help and blessings, but when one gr
the position at all cost, the position becomes a scorching fire to the (
who grabs it.

Friend, always remember this (especially when it involves
Church): Take and hold does not mean take for keeps (*nara jiji ab*
nara were). We do not remove our caps for one because one has deci
to run amok in the Church (*obughi onye baa mba, ekpupuru ya okp*
When it comes to choosing and having servant-leaders at all levels of
church, let sanity reign in the Church of Christ!

Let us Pray:

Almighty and provident father, in Ex. 18:21 when you ch
Moses as leader of your people of Israel, you blessed him with al
God-fearing and trustworthy men to help him shepherd your flo
and in Acts 6:3-4, you also blessed the Apostles with reputable, H
Spirit-filled and wise men to help them shepherd your flock.

You have also through generations of Church history contin
to bless your Church with men and women who help your Past
in shepherding your flock in the administration of various fa
communities. Continue to make them able, God-fearing, trustwort
reputable, Spirit-filled and wise men and women in your vineyard

We make this prayer through our Lord Jesus Christ, your son v
lives and reigns with you, in the unity of the Holy Spirit, one C
forever and ever. Amen!

7. Ezekiel 37:12-14; Romans 8:8-11; John 11:1-45

We Die To Live!

Friend, we die to live; we do not die to die. In the Prophecy of ekiel, God says: Oh my people, I will open your graves and have u rise from them…because the Spirit of God, which I will put in u (and which according to the text of Romans is already in us), is onger than death.

Jesus, therefore, says emphatically to us this Lent as he said Martha over 2000 years ago: "I am the resurrection and the life; oever believes in me, even if he dies, will live, and everyone who es and believes in me will never die" (John 11:26).

No founder of any other religion has ever made such an assertion claimed such power over death. What does this tell you about us? Who could make such statement? Who has the power to make e tomb empty?

In the biblical encounter with the Samaritan woman at Jacob's Well hn 4:5-42), Jesus is the Living water: to quench our spiritual thirst. the biblical encounter with the man born blind (John 9:1-41), Jesus he Light of the world: to dispel our spiritual blindness. In the above lical text of John, which narrates the encounter between Martha d Mary at the funeral of Lazarus, Jesus is the Resurrection and the e: to give immortality to our mortality, to give imperishability to r perishability, to give eternity to our temporality.

So I make out of all these that Jesus my Savior came into this World quench my spiritual thirst, to throw light into the blind spots of my e, and to give immortality and imperishability to my mortal and rishable body. WOW…. I AM BLESSED! And you are blessed too, / friend! Indeed we are all blessed because as Christians we are in is together.

And if I really understand this, I will joyously continue to seek us Christ every day.

Yet, the omnipotence of God reigns, not only over my ultimate rtal death, but also over all other little deaths I have to experience

in life, things I have to grieve for: bad health, job loss, insecur
wounded relationships, etc. Count your crosses, name them one
one. In all these little deaths, God can also bring life out of death.

Friend, at this juncture, let each one ask himself/herself th
questions:

• What in my life must die in order for God to bring about n
life in me?

• Are there graves in my life I need to be raised from?

• Are there bindings in my life Christ has to free me from?

As Christians, let us always remember that at Baptism, we died
old ways that are ungodly and, therefore, we should seek every day
grow in the new life that Jesus Christ has won for us.

Romans 8:28 says: "We know that all things work for good
those who love God"

May this blessed hope continue to give life to our Souls. Amen

Ezekiel 2:2-5; 2Cor 12:7-10; Mark 6:1-6

We are All Human!

Friend, in the scripture text of 2 Corinthians, Apostle Paul says: thorn in the flesh was given me.... Three times I begged the Lord this to leave me, but he said to me: my grace is sufficient for you, power is made perfect in weakness". There are speculations on what is thorn in the flesh of Apostle Paul could be. Is it referring to his ers or his epilepsy? Whatever that thorn is, Paul knows.

The important message, however, is that it reminds you and I of human condition: No matter how pretty, how beautiful, and how ly we may look from the outside, each of us carries something inside our stomach) that stenches; and no matter how accomplished one ght be, there might still be areas in one's life that seek answers.

This brings us to the issue of faith in the Gospel text of Mark 6:1- The people of Nazareth are not impressed at Jesus' profile, and they ked faith. The very circumstances of Jesus' humble background, wever, reminds us that it is not only the intellectually gifted, or financially successful, or the politically strong, who can make a ference in society; indeed we all can contribute to the wellbeing society no matter our earthly status. This Gospel presents the sad ory of people who met with Jesus and left without a blessing. When wonder of God's inaction at happenings here below, is God not azed and appalled at our unbelief (Cf. Mark 6:6).

Friend, one of the most shocking statements in the Gospels is that us could not perform miracles, not that he would not but that he nply could not. Is anything impossible for God? This Gospel passage ms to suggest "yes" to the question: Yes, it is impossible for God to rform miracles in situations where there is no faith. Jesus could do things, and wants to do all things, but he needs our faith to release power. Do you remember the Gospel story of the woman with the ue of blood (Cf. Mark 5:21-43); people are pushing and touching us and nothing is happening, but as soon as the woman of faith ches Him, healing power comes out of Jesus. Faith is like a switch t turns God on! Familiarity, indeed, can bring contempt; we see this in Jesus' people of Nazareth.

The tear in the flesh of Paul reminds us that we are all hum who are in dire need of grace; and the Gospel encounter challen us to strive every day to reach out in faith to God to discover a understand the new things that God is offering us through the sa old and familiar channels.

As we meet God each day in his word and in his sacraments, n we continue to renew our faith and leave each divine encounter w blessings. Amen!

God's Crosses for Me and the Crosses I Create for Myself

Friend, the first part of the scripture text from the Epistle of St. Peter 3-16 tells us that we are united with Christ through our sufferings for m and his Gospel. But the second part of the same Scripture text warn to ensure that the crosses we bear are the ones God has allowed us to rry for there could be crosses that are not allowed by God but emanate m our human miscalculations.

Jesus says: "My yoke is easy and my burden light". We must, therefore, tinguish between the Crosses (sufferings) God has allowed us to carry d the crosses we may have created for ourselves out of our carelessness d recklessness. Let me give one example:

A man (or woman) abandons his or her family responsibilities (God's sses), gets involved in marital infidelity and eventually contacts philis through extra-marital affairs. In his suffering, he goes to the apel, and before the Blessed Sacrament prays: "Jesus, remove this cross philis) from me for it is eating me up". Jesus responds: "No! This is t my cross. It is your cross. You created and entrusted this cross upon urself, bear the burden".

This may sound funny. But friend, there are certain responsibilities d has placed upon our shoulders in the family, in the Church, and in larger society, and he will never allow them to overwhelm us. But we ist avoid creating unnecessary crosses for ourselves.

In the Gospel text of John 17:1-11[a], Jesus talks of "His hour". What this "Jesus' hour"? It is his hour of suffering and glorification. We all ist participate in this "Jesus' hour" for where there is no cross, there is crown.

The second part of this Gospel text affirms that eternal life is to know only true God and Jesus Christ whom he sent. "Knowing God is t exactly the same as "believing in God". Knowing God is personal; owing God is intimate; knowing God is relational.

To get to this personal intimate relationship, the Apostles in the mpany of Mary the Mother of Jesus prayed for the "Spirit of the Living

God" (Acts1:12-24). Friend, to be united with God in prayer, we ne
the Holy Spirit; to be united to Jesus' hour of suffering and glorificati
we need the holy Spirit; to be able to carry the Crosses God has allow
to be placed on our shoulders and to avoid creating unnecessary ones
ourselves, we need the Holy Spirit; to know God in a personal intim
relationship, we need the Holy Spirit.

Let us pray: Come Holy Spirit fill the hearts of the faithful, enkin
in them the fire of thy love. Amen!

Isaiah 42:1-4, 6-7; Acts 10:34-38; Mark 1:7-11

Let's Go About Doing Good!

Friend, did Jesus need to be baptized? Yes, as Son of Man, he needed During his ministry on Earth, Jesus used words, actions and gestures teach us about God's kingdom and the ways of God unto salvation. John 3:5, Jesus underscores the importance of "Water Baptism". In e Gospel (Matt 3:13-17; Mark 1:9-12; Luke 3:21-22; Cf. John 1:26, 32-) Jesus was baptized and at his baptism we notice the presence of the ily Trinity (Father, Son and Holy Spirit) as evidence of New Creation Grace (Cf. Genesis 1:2; John 1:37). In John 3: 22, 26, Jesus himself ptized people. In Matthew 28:19, Jesus gives the Church the mandate baptize and the format for baptism.

After the baptism of Jesus by John the Baptist with water from River rdan, what was next for Jesus? Acts of the Apostles tells us that "Jesus nt about doing good…." (Acts 10:38). This means that baptism is the ginning of what God is doing in us, and the beginning of what God uld use us to do in the lives of others (Mmirichukwu bu mmalite ihe ukwu n'aru n'ime mmadu, nakwa mmalite ihe Chukwu g'eji mmadu 1 n'ebe ndi ozo no)

Friend, to be able to inherit Heaven, we must get involved in renewing e earth, in making society a good place to live and enjoy God's peace. id this is precisely what each Christian is called to do in our family cles, and then extend it to our communities and society at large. HE ENT ABOUT DOING GOOD!

To make our society good for all of us is never the responsibility of the w; it is the responsibility of all, more or less. In this we are all producers d consumers: producers of the good and consumers of the good. The ture in which God comes and which we hope for (Heaven) does not ustrate the present in which man and woman lives (our world). This ture (which we all are seeking) is realized in our responsible availability the present. HE WENT ABOUT DOING GOOD!

Friend and beloved in Christ, there is no room, therefore, for iritual dormancy for a baptized person. We all have to become tive in the society. We all must get involved in making our families, our communities, our neighborhoods and the society in which we l habitable.

May the Lord's baptism renew our own baptism and rekindle c sense of purpose and innate resolve to partake in God's work of renew the face of the earth. Having been baptized into Christ's death, may also share in his resurrection and newness of life. Amen!

Acts 10:37-43; Colossians 3:1-4; Matthew 28:1-10

The Lord is Risen and We are Witnesses

Friend, every Good Friday we usually chant this hymn:

Were you there when they crucified my Lord? / Were you there when *y crucified my Lord? / Oh, sometimes it causes me to tremble, tremble,* *mble. / Were you there when they crucified my Lord? / Were you there* *en they nailed Him to the tree? / Were you there when they nailed him* *the tree? / Oh, sometimes it causes me to tremble, tremble, tremble. /* *re you there when they nailed him to the tree?*

Our long journey of Lent and Holy Week happily ends with Easter: Resurrection of Jesus. His resurrection is the reason for the Faith that have (I Cor 15:14, 17).

Hymn: He's alive, amen; He's alive; Jesus is alive forever, He's alive, en!

The four versions of the Gospel of our Lord Jesus Christ have accounts the resurrection of Jesus. I am particularly thrilled by some incidents the above Gospel account of Mathew: it is Matthew who tells us that en Jesus died, there was an Earthquake (Matt 27:510; Matthew tells there was another earthquake when Jesus rose from the dead (Matt :2): this is to let us know that Jesus' death and resurrection are two smic events that shook the foundations of the world and split history o BC and AD making Jesus the center point of history.

It is Matthew who tells us of the powerful Roman guards who were ghtened and were like dead men before the angels: this is to let us ow that worldly powers are no match for Heavenly powers, the powers God.

It is Matthew who tells us that the women were made announcers of resurrection first by the two angels, and later by the Risen Jesus: as it re as a reward for their courage in coming to see the tomb.

Be that as it may, the text of Acts 10 affirms that all of us are now tnesses of the Easter good news: witnesses to the good news of divine tice (that evil is punished and good is rewarded); witnesses to the

good news of divine reconciliation (which has made it possible
all of us to be under the one roof, called the Church, as brothers
sisters in Christ and calls us to embrace one another with open min
witnesses to divine peace (peace in our hearts that calls us to reject
forms of violence and wars); witnesses of divine mercy (which invite
to bear with one another and resist being harsh in judging one anoth
witnesses of divine love (that reaches out without borders).
resurrection power must, therefore, manifest in us, in our lives, in w
we think, in what we do, and in what we say. The resurrection po
must enlighten our minds, direct our thoughts and influence our actic
If the resurrection power is at work in us, we must become enthusia
about praying, we must become enthusiastic about the word of G
we must become enthusiastic about receiving Jesus in the Euchar
we must become enthusiastic about faith activities in community
fellowshipping with others, we must become enthusiastic about shar
our faith with others; we must become bold and courageous in do
these without allowing ourselves to be intimidated by those who do
want to hear about God, about Christ and about the Church; we m
begin to hate sin and become sincere in living the Christian life (
Acts 2:42). In this way, we will be moving away from a dead or dorm
faith to a living faith. A living faith meets God in the Scriptures; a liv
faith worships the Lord in the liturgy and the sacraments; a living fa
serves the Lord in ministry to others; a living faith shines out life-l
commitments; a living faith responds to socio-cultural, socio-politi
and socio-economic obligations; a living faith speaks and shares
goodness of God.

These are the real challenges of Easter. In these and other ways,
glory of the resurrection continues to be manifest in our World. Th
are the ways we keep our eyes and hearts on the things of Heaven as
Scripture text of Colossians invites us to do.

When we come to Holy Mass, the Risen Christ is truly present in
assembly in His Word and in the Sacrament. Every Holy Mass Celebra
and re-enacts the Easter mystery. Through the Word and the Euchar
may our risen Lord continue to help us to be vibrant witnesses of div
justice, peace, reconciliation, mercy and love. Amen!

Sirach 15:15-20; 1Cor 2:6-10; Matt 5:17-37

Freedom of Choice & Responsibility

Friend, Ben Sirach (180 years before Christ) teaches on freedom. this "land of the free and home of the brave", Sirach reminds us t freedom defined as right to choose comes with responsibility. reminds us that God does not understand freedom or liberty as nse to do whatever one wants (Is 15:20). In order words, whatever one's choices, one should be ready to accept the present and eternal nsequences as they come.

Apostle Paul in the scripture text from the book of Corinthians ds that practice of freedom of choice should go with maturity.

Jesus in the Gospel passage of Matthew emphasizes that our edom of choice must always be guided by a Christian maturity t attaches much importance to the interior state of our minds and nsciences, especially on issues of purity, decency, truthfulness, nesty and justice in relating to others. Jesus pins down the whole essage of today on love: that we must love others so much that we uld not even want to harm them, as he has also won us the grace practice this.

The truth is that whenever we feel we are smarter than God and cide to make and follow our own rules as Adam and Eve did in n, we face disaster. However, we must be careful not to condemn rselves when negative feelings as anger, envy, greed, pride, lust, iness or whatever negative impulse may have made a way into us. w we respond to these negative impulses and feelings or instinct what is important to God and to our salvation. Rain must fall and od must flow, but it is left for the owner of the house to channel flood so that it does not enter the House and do damage (*Mmiri zoriri, Mmiri ide g'ehuriri,mana obu onye new ulo k'odiri igbopu ide oghara ibata n'ulo mebie ihe*).

Commenting on these Scripture texts, CCC n.1972 has this to : "The New Law is called a *law of love* because it makes us act out the love infused by the Holy Spirit, rather than from fear; a *law grace*, because it confers the strength of grace to act, by means of

faith and the sacraments; a *law of freedom*, because it sets us free fr
the ritual and juridical observances of the Old Law, inclines us to
spontaneously by the prompting of charity…"

Let us pray to live this law of Christian Love, this law of Redempt
Grace, and this law of Responsible Freedom every day and in
situations – Amen!

. 1Kgs 19:9^b, 11^b-12, 13^b; I Cor 4:6^b-15; Rev. 4:1-11

...rough Holy Sound, We Touch God, and We Touch Lives Too

Friend, in the Scripture text from St. Paul's letter to the Church in ...rinth, the question is asked: What do we possess that we have not ...eived from the Lord? What vocation? What carrier? What talent? ...at hobby? The Psalmist clearly understands that who he is and what ... possesses are gifts from God, and that is why he proclaims: "May ... mouth sing the praise of the Lord; and may all my flesh bless his ...ly name forever and ever". This understanding and disposition of the ...lmist is the understanding and disposition of every Christian when, ...en, with our lips and hearts, we resound praises unto the lord.

Friend, in a spirit of adoration through sacred and liturgical music, ...especially touch God, and touch lives too.

From the Scripture text of Kings chapter 19, we learn that through ...red music, we invoke God who moves through holy sound: "At ... Mount of God, Horeb...a strong and heavy wind was rending the ...untains and crushing rocks, but the Lord was not in the wind. After ... wind there was an earthquake, but the Lord was not in the earthquake. ...d after the earthquake there was fire, but the Lord was not in the fire. ...er the fire, there was a tiny whispering sound...and God spoke to ...n". God was not in the tornado, was not in the earthquake, was not ...the fire; but in the tiny whispering sound, Elijah heard God's voice. ...end, this holy sound is epitomized in sacred and liturgical music ...ich we devotedly render to God in the Church.

Again, from Joshua chapter 6, Numbers chapter 20 and Acts chapter ... we learn that through sacred music, we invoke God whose Spirit, ...ce, blessing, miraculous presence and deliverance move through ...ly sound. In Joshua 6, God asks Joshua and the people of Israel to ...ve around the walls of Jericho seven times sounding the trumpet, ...1 the walls of Jericho would crumble and God's people would move ...o the land of promise. Through the sounding of the trumpet, and ...hout firing a bullet, the walls gave way and the people moved in. In ...mbers chapter 20, King Jehoshaphat of Judah faces the hostility from

the kingdoms of Ammon, Moab and Edom as they connive to att
and wage war against Judah. God instructs Jehoshaphat: "This ba
is not yours but mine…. See the deliverance the Lord will give y
March out against them, but you will not need to fight the battle
[15,16,17]). Jehoshaphat appointed men to sing to the Lord and praise l
for the splendor of His Holiness saying: "Give thanks to the Lord
His love endures forever". As they began to sing and praise, the L
set ambushes against the men of Ammon and Moab…and they w
defeated. They fought and destroyed one another. The men of Judah
only dead bodies…no one escaped" (Vs [21,22,23]). Friend, do you no
that the soldiers of Judah did not fire even a bullet, they only sang
praised the splendor of God's Holiness and God delivered them fr
the multitudes of a raging army. In Acts 16, while Paul and Barna
are in prison, we hear them praying and singing while other prisor
listen to them. And God comes with a land tremor to fling the dc
open, loosen the chains and frees everyone: God, indeed, moves thro
Holy sound. Friend, transforming movements of the Holy Spirit, g
miracles, untold deliverances, and incalculable healings happen w
God's children open their lips and hearts to praise God who mc
through holy sound, especially sacred music.

Then comes the most important: We learn from Revelations chap
4 that through sacred music, we acknowledge and proclaim the splen
of God's holiness. This passage talks of the vision by Apostle John
God's throne in Heaven where he sees the 24 elders (V[4]) and the 4 liv
creatures "worshipping day and night without ceasing singing H
Holy Holy is the Lord God Almighty who was, and is, and is to cc
(V[8])….You are worthy, our Lord and God, to receive glory and ho
and power, for you created all things, and by your will they were crea
and have their being (V[11])".

Friend, while still on earth, we already participate in this heave
liturgy and eternal worship of God through sacred music. On earth,
in the Church are for God the 24 elders, the four living creatures,
angels and the multitude of saints singing before God's throne. What
I say friend: Keep the flame of faith burning; rise and shine in prais
God unceasingly for God's anointing is upon you. Amen!

. Leviticus 19:1-2, 17-18; 1Cor 3:16-23; Luke 6:27-38

Holy Holy Holy (*Nso Nso Nso*)

In the Scripture text from Leviticus 19:2, we read "Holy"; in the text ›m 1 Cor 3:17, we read "Holy"; and in the Gospel text from Matthew ·8, we read "Holy". In the three scripture texts we have "Holy Holy ›ly". This reminds us of the *Sanctus Sanctus Sanctus* that we usually ⸋laim at every Holy Mass (Eucharistic celebration). Friend, how does ₊e become holy? Holiness is not acquired but given (received) as a gift.

The book of Leviticus (the 3rd book of the Old Testament) deals ₊ensively on holiness, Priesthood and temple worship "Be holy for I ₊ur God am holy". Holiness is whole ness; being holy is being whole.

In the Gospel according to Matthew, Jesus continues the sermon ₊the Mount which is an interpretation of the holiness precept of ₊viticus. In addition to purity, decency, honesty, truthfulness, justice, ₊us adds self-control and love as signs of our maturity in Christ which ₊called holiness, wholeness. On self-control and love, Christ enjoins ₊t Christians should not be vengeful but love even when we are struck. ₊n't strike anybody whether by physical or verbal combat: BE GOOD! ₊manly speaking, this is one of the most difficult demands by Christ ₊ Christians. By every human standard and judgment, it is madness. ₊wever, Jesus himself gives us "the reason" and "the blessing" for ₊h a difficult demand. The reason: Because we are the children of the ₊avenly father who causes his sun to shine for the good and the bad, ₊ꓱ makes his rain fall for the good and the bad (Cf. Lk 6:35); and the ₊ssing: if we do, we will enjoy God's unmitigated love, kindness and ₊ꓱevolence (Cf. Lk. 6:37-38).

The Apostle states in James 1:15 -- "When anger reaches maturity, it ₊es birth to death".

I said it to you friend as I say to many, beware of anger, be it in your ₊ꓲe, be it in the Church, anywhere and anytime, because anger comes ₊h a chain of evil if untamed: Anger (iwe) leads to misunderstanding ₊ꓴuko), and misunderstanding leads to dispute (esemokwu), and dispute ₊ꓓ to Resentment (mkpomasi), and resentment leads to bitterness/ ₊ter spirit (obi ilu), and bitterness leads to murder (igbu ochu).

Do you see why Blessed Apostle in the text from 1 Corinthi
warns that to destroy any person in any way is to be guilty of destroy
God's Holy Temple. It is because of anger that some of us go on harm
and destroying others. Do you get from this text how God will reac
any person who does this?

To remain holy, therefore, we must manage our anger, instin
temperament and outbursts well with vigilance so that we do not si
is true that certain negative feelings and instincts are natural to huma
But they must be tamed: rain must come, floods must flow, but it ta
the owner of the house to control the flood so that it does no damag
the house. When anger reaches maturity, it gives birth to death.

Let's hear what the CCC nn. 1968, and 1825 says on today's readi
2844

1968: The Law of the Gospel *fulfils the commandments* of the L
The Lord's Sermon on the Mount, far from abolishing or devaluing
moral prescriptions of the Old Law, releases their hidden potential
has new demands arise from them: it reveals their entire divine
human truth. It does not add new external precepts, but proceed
reform the heart, the root of human acts, where man chooses betw
the pure and the impure,[22] where faith, hope, and charity are forr
and with them the other virtues. The Gospel thus brings the Law
its fullness through imitation of the perfection of the heavenly Fat
through forgiveness of enemies and prayer for persecutors, in emulat
of the divine generosity.

2844: Christian prayer extends to the *forgiveness of enemie*
transfiguring the disciple by configuring him to his Master. Forgiver
is a high-point of Christian prayer; only hearts attuned to G
compassion can receive the gift of prayer. Forgiveness also bears wit
that, in our world, love is stronger than sin. The martyrs of yester
and today bear this witness to Jesus. Forgiveness is the fundame
condition of the reconciliation of the children of God with their Fat
and of men with one another.

1825: Christ died out of love for us, while we were still "enemies
The Lord asks us to love as he does, even our *enemies*, to make ourse
the neighbor of those farthest away, and to love children and the poo
Christ himself.

May the Holy Spirit continue to help us overcome certain instincts, nperaments, inclinations and appetites that prevent us from growing holiness or attaining wholeness in Christ and in the Holy Eucharist. y we continue to be transformed into who we receive. Amen! HOLY)LY HOLY (Nso Nso Nso)!

95. Exodus 34: 4b-6, 8-9; 2Cor 13:11-13; John 3:18-18

Trinity and Fathers

In the name of the father and of the Son and of the Holy Spirit, Am

Trinity was first used by Tertulian to describe the three person one God in the year. 200 AD. The term was officially adopted by Council of Nicea 125 years later in the Nicene Creed. The dogma on trinity is one of the cardinal teachings and principles of our Christ faith

Friend, Jesus, the second person of the Trinity, who gave Christianity revealed the trinity in a tangible way at his baptism w the Father spoke from heaven and the Spirit descended. Jesus also s that "he and the Father are one" (Jn 10:30). Jesus also said, "he who s me has seen the father (14:9). By Jesus' command, we have been bapti "in the name of the father and of the son and of the holy Spirit (M 28:19). Jesus also taught us call God father (Matt 6:9).

At Holy Mass as in other Christian prayer, we direct our prayer the Father "Through our Lord Jesus Christ who lives and reigns with Father in the unity of the Holy Spirit, one God forever and ever".

The first person of the Trinity is Father. In the text of Exodus, C the Father reveals himself to Moses as: "merciful, gracious, slow to an rich in kindness and fidelity". Junior was observing bedtime prayer w his Dad. At a point, Junior asked the dad to leave so that he could tall God alone. The mesmerized Dad retorted: Junior, what have you d that you wouldn't want me to know? (*Jr gini ka i mere i n'achoghi k Mara?*) Junior replied, Dad, if I tell you now, you will become angry, yell, you shout. But if I tell God, he listens to me, he embraces me, shows me mercy (*M koro gi ugbua, i wewe iwe, bawa mba, tiwe mk Ma M koro chukwu nna, o gere M nti,nabata M, gbaghara M*).

Whenever we celebrate Mothers, the model that readily come mind is the Immaculate Virgin Mary. But when we celebrate Fath the model is Blessed St. Joseph: an obedient servant of God, a dedica husband of Mary, a hardworking carpenter who did his best to supp his family and support God's cause (not one who will be playing dra me waiting for the wife to bring home bunches of money), a husband d father whose vocation to marriage and family life is more important n career or business.

I plead with Fathers as pillars of your families: continue to love d protect your families from physical, moral and spiritual dangers, ntinue to take interest in knowing what your kids watch on television d the Internet, continue to take interest in knowing what your ds' temperaments, inclinations, habits and choices are, continue to e interest in knowing who your kids' friends are, continue to take erest in knowing what your children think about important moral ues, continue to take interest in preparing your kids to face the moral allenges and temptations of life, and continue to take interest in ching them about the faith that you have.

Fathers, you're not only the pillars of your families, you are also the lars of our community: the tempo of our Community is set by what ppens amongst you! What happens among you affects our children d determines the tempo of their relationships with one another (*ndi a noro n'ogu na mgba, ebe nile ga n'esi Ogu na mgba Ogu na mgba*).

In the spirit of the text from 2Cor 13:11-13, Let's cultivate peace d love; let each of you seek to stop the hate culture being spread all und; learn to encourage one another rather than fight one another; rn to work together rather than undo one another; learn to promote e another rather than destroy one another; learn to promote peace her than insinuate infighting. Fathers and men, reduce the strife ongst you and in your groups and create an environment of peace our children to grow. Let us help our children to avoid the rough and ly path of bitter rivalry and wickedness so that when we tell these our ldren to appreciate our culture, they will take us seriously and follow cause we are leading.

Our Fathers and Men, as critical figures in your families, and in our mmunity and in our Church, we cannot do without you. That is why appreciate you all today, pray for you, and say Thank You!

I invoke upon you our fathers and men the blessings of God the her, Son and Holy Spirit and the patronage of Blessed St. Joseph. EN!

96.   Acts 6:1-7; 1Peter 2:4-9; John 14:1-12

Keeping Before You the "Bigger Picture"

Friend, in the early chapters of Acts, Luke presents to us a peace harmonious and progressive community of Christians growing in fa hope, love and numbers, and without internal problems. But that i community of one culture: Jews who spoke Hebrew and Aramaic. I in Acts 6, the Christian community grows larger. And internal proble surface:

** First, Doctrinal: Cultural complication of how to admit conve from other parts of the Roman empire of Hellenistic culture who sp the common language of the empire, Greek, was handled by the doctri definition of the 1st Council of Jerusalem.

** Second, Social Justice: Economic discrimination in the neglec Christian widows of Greek origin in the sharing of food was hand through creation of the office of the diaconate.

Friend, listen to this: To resolve the issues that arose, the Commur recommended seven persons and the Apostles (leaders) confirmed a appointed them deacons to serve the community and ensure equity a fairness. And so has the Holy Spirit always helped the church throu the centuries to handle issues that arose in the church.

Friend, issues of concern in the church, internal problems, corrections to be made, are handled, not through activism, but throu attentive prayer and discernment that proffer appropriate soluti according to the signs of the times. Yet, no matter the issues, no ma the concerns, no matter the problems, no matter the crisis, no matter ups and downs, Jesus tells us: *Do not let your hearts be troubled. I am way and the truth and the life.* But we cannot but be troubled the m when we use this categorical statement of Jesus as a mirror to look at world:

** *I am the way* in a world where many seem to have lost their wa

** *I am the truth* in a world that is invaded by falsehoods and falsit

** *I am the life* in a world where the culture of death (wars, violer rorism, kidnapping, militancy) overwhelms the culture of life?

Some people in our world today would even want us to believe that
r world does not need God anymore and that we should do away with
d and the things of God.

But the truth is that since today many people have lost their way,
ice falsehoods and falsities have invaded our world, since the culture
death is having a field day, we need God in our world and in our
arts more than ever, contrary to the opinion of some who tell us we
n't need God anymore. The statement of Jesus in the Gospel of John
apter 14 (I am....), therefore, which is an urgent summoning to us to
n back to God is as valid today as ever. Jesus encourages us not to be
scouraged or troubled or overwhelmed by what we see in our world.
d is still in control and there comes a time when all who walk the way
God, seek the truth of God, and live the life of God, will be rewarded
heaven. But he reminds us too that the way to this heaven is not a
eet you can walk through, is not a driveway you can cruise on, is not
lapQuest you can Google that tells you how to get there. No! The way
heaven is a person, Jesus Christ himself, the way and the truth and the
, who according to 1 Peter chapter 2, builds us in the Church into a
ritual house for God.

Friend, as we deal with the ups and downs of life, the word of God
ites us to keep before us daily the Big Picture: "I am going to prepare a
ce for you...and I will come back to take you...so that where I am, you
o may be". And we say to this promise, Amen!

97. Acts 12:1-11; 2Tim 4:6-8, 17-18; Matt 16:13-19

SAINTS PETER AND PAUL: LEADERSHIP & CHARIS

Friend, each year we celebrate Peter and Paul, we come face to f with leadership and charism in the church. In celebrating these t apostolic pillars of the Church together, the Church recalls:

**not only the fact that they worked harmoniously together to bu up the Church in the two important areas of leadership and charism:

**not only the fact that the two of them suffered martyrdom in Ro during the persecution of emperor Nero;

**but most importantly they remind us of the importance leadership and guidance in the Church on the one hand, as well charisma for ministry or service in the Church, on the other hand.

The position of Peter, as indicated in the Gospel passage accord to Apostle Matthew, reminds us that leadership and guidance a exists in the Church is according to the intention of Christ. Yes, we are members of the Church, but there is always a leader and guide (*eziokwu na anyi Nile bucha ndi uka ndi uka, mana enwere Onye bu O isi na onye ndu ebe obula igara*). And though this leading and guid voice of the Church subsists strongly with the Bishop of Rome (Po| because of the unity and universality of the Church, it does not stop w him but runs down the line of the Church's hierarchy. For example:

**universal level: Pope is this leading and guiding voice for Church;

**particular Church level: Cardinal Sean O'Malley is this lead and guiding voice for the church in the Roman Catholic Archdioces Boston;

**Parish level: Pastor Jerry Osterman is this leading and guid voice for the Church in St. Katharine Drexel Parish, Boston.

Moving further in our discussion on leadership and charism, position of Paul reminds the rest of us that to the leading and guid voices of the church, we all are helpers and collaborators through various charisms or gifts for ministry and service in the Church. '

ly Spirit helps to release our gifts and make them available for the wth of the Church.

Always remember this: Paul respected the leader role of Peter in the urch and Peter recognized the charisms for mission in Paul.

Let us pray that through the intercessions of Saints Peter and Paul, may become more docile to, and respectful of the voice of leadership d guidance in our Church. Let us be more enabled and empowered to ply our God-given gifts for the salvation of many. Amen!

98.   Deut 6:4-8; Colossians 1:6; Matt 13:18-23

HEARING AND UNDERSTANDING GOD'S WORD

Friend, I have in my Parish community the life testimony of a parishioner, Andrew, of a spiritual turnaround in his life and how things started turning out good in his life after he started taking God's Word seriously. Until this transformation, he had attended Church for 35 years, but all this while, he had no appetite for word of God and nothing positive seemed to have happened in life. Andrew used to shop for neighborhood Parishes where priest gave the shortest homilies and his idea of a good Sunday service was one that took as little time as possible. Since his transformation 1 years ago after 35yrs, Andrew can now listen to homilies with and can testify to the richness of the Word. He has also become member of the parish Bible study group where I am the founder spiritual director.

Our disposition for the Word of God is a good indication of relationship with him. The parable of the sower in the Gospel lik the teaching of the Word of God to sowing of seeds. The seeds on different types of soil: the pathway soil, the rocky soil, the tho soil, and the good soil. Each of these types of soil is said to repres a certain type of heart with which hearers receive the word of Go

Listen to Jesus (Mt 13:19): "When anyone hears the Word the Kingdom and does not understand it, the evil one comes snatches away what is sown in the heart, that is what's on path And Jesus says in Matt 13:23: "But as for what was sown on good s this is the one who hears the Word and understands it, who ind bears fruit...."

What is it that makes one person understand and another per not understand the Gospel? Disposition. And we go back to Andr All the 35 years he was not disposed, the Word of God made no se to him. The Word of God became meaningful and fruitful to from the moment he disposed himself to God.

Friend, to the person who is properly disposed to the Word of d, the Word brings about abundant fruits. But for the person who ll-disposed to the Word of God, the word is dead on arrival. But member Col 1:6: "the Gospel is being preached throughout the rld and is bringing blessings".

Let us individually ask for the grace to be always properly disposed God's Word so as to continue to reap the blessings therein. Amen!

99. Isaiah 55:1-3; Romans 8:35, 37-39; Matt 14:13-21

WE COME TO GOD TO BE BLESSED AND NOT TO BE CURSED

After 50 years of exile in Babylon, God through prophet Isaiah t the people of Israel that they will again drink water and milk from tl own land, and eat corn and wheat from their own farms and that he restore them.

Friend, the scripture texts from Isaiah, the Psalm and the Go: according to Apostle Matthew remind us of one of the reasons why come to God: We come to God to be blessed by him, we do not com him to be cursed; and we go better for it! We come to God for all posi reasons: to be counselled, to be taught, to be liberated, to be delivered be healed, to be fed, etc.

Roman 8 tells us that is why no sane person would walk away fi God, from Jesus Christ, and from his Church for any reason. In Mattl 22: 1-14 (parable of the king who gave a wedding banquet for his son) see many gave reasons and walked away. In Matthew 13: 44-46 (par; of the hidden treasure), we see two groups of people in our world tod those who sell off all they have to possess God, salvation, heaven, those who sell out God, salvation, heaven to get all that they want.

Friend, we are Christians: the group of people, I hope, who ready to sell off all they have in order to buy the greatest treasure: C Salvation, heaven. This means that as Christians, our greatest prio should be to please God, to be saved, to go to heaven. Other things instruments to help us attain this priority.

May the counsels of God, his teaching, his liberation and heali and the feeding that we receive from him, especially in the Eucha help each one of us to attain that greatest good which is the salvatio our souls. Amen!

0. Zechariah 9:9-10; Romans 8:9, 11-13; Matt 11:25-30

FREEDOM

Friend, to be free is a sweet experience. We celebrate each year the niversaries of independence of our various nations; and we still hope better days ahead.

In the Scripture text from Prophet Zachariah, it has been 300 years Israel's freedom from the brutal Babylonian captivity, and yet God omises through the Prophet better days of freedom and peace for usalem. Jesus tells us in Matthew 10:28: "Do not be afraid of those o kill the body but can't kill the soul. Rather, be afraid of the one o can destroy both soul and body in hell". That's why in the Gospel itation of Jesus: "Come to me all you who labor and are burdened, d I will give you rest", Jesus offers us a freedom far above that from our litical, economic and cultural slave masters: Jesus himself becomes r resting place.

It is in Jesus that we experience our true freedom. When we come to us, the text of Romans tells us that the Spirit of God sets us free from r interior slavery to evil choices, evil inclinations, evil temperaments, d evil attitudes, and gives us peace. Jesus says in Romans 8:36: 'hoever the Son of God sets free is free indeed".

Friend, the message is that as we continue to work hard for freedom m whatever would continue to enslave us politically, economically, turally, we must also work harder by God's grace to free ourselves m whatever lifestyles that would enslave us spiritually. In this way, our edom will be complete. We at least know one truth: things are not yet rfect, and our nations are not yet perfect. Let us continue to pray and rk with God for a more just and peaceful society and world.

Jesus speaks to you and I today: "My yoke is easy and my burden ht".

Amen!

101. Jeremiah 20:7-9; Romans 12:1-2; Matt 16:21-27

UNEASY CALL, UNPOPULAR MESSAGE

HYMN: *Eburula M obe nwanne M amalitela M ikpe ekpe Eburula M obe*

obe Jesu

Jesus says to Peter (not told Peter); "Go behind me, Satan". is, therefore, not calling Peter Satan; Jesus is rather referring another being outside of Peter that might be trying to use him distract him from his predestined mission.

Friend, when Jeremiah was called,(c.600bc), he had thought t the work would be easy. But he was caught up in a vocation wher he was to sell an unpopular message which made him unpopu too and brought him suffering. He was hated, ridiculed, jailed, a thrown into the muddy cistern to die.

Again, as we read in the gospel according to Matthew, mission of Jesus would also bring him suffering and death.

During electioneering campaigns, politicians turn our natio into "lands of promise", promising us all the goodies that sou good to our ears. Jesus on the contrary promises an agenda that v be tough both for him and for his followers.

Friend, Jesus did not come to bring us suffering, or to tell that it is good to suffer. He came to establish God's Kingdom that we may "have life and have it more abundantly" (John 10:1 When Jesus invites us to carry our crosses daily and follow h he is reminding us that there are some crosses, some sufferings cannot avoid on the way of our journey to God: sufferings fr our responsibilities to family (family commitments), sufferi from our responsibilities to others and to society (socio-cultu engagements), and sufferings from our responsibilities to C (church obligations). These sufferings and crosses bring us clo to Christ who carried a cross for us. This is why we begin and e every Holy Mass with the sign of the cross.

At each Holy Mass we attend, we recall Jesus' love and sacrifice
us. It is especially at Holy Mass that Jesus gives us strength to
low him carrying our crosses, as, according to Romans 12:2, we
er ourselves and our spiritual worship to him "as living sacrifice,
ly and pleasing to God. Amen!

102. Isaiah 56:1, 6-7; Rom 11:13-15, 29-32; Matt 15:21-2

MIRACLE, MENTALITY, PRAYER

Mentality, Miracle, Prayer: These are the themes that come prominently in these scripture readings.

In Isaiah, we read: "Foreigners who join themselves to the L administering to him, loving his name and becoming his servants, Will Bless!" The question is: WHO ARE THESE FOREIGNERS? prophecy of Isaiah chapter 56 is coming from the background of Isr rejection of Gentiles (*Ndi mba ozo*), that the Gentiles (non-Jews) h no share in the promises and blessings of God.

Jesus is very much aware of this mentality. You can now see setting for the most humiliating (though most saving) encounter the Gospel according to Matthew between Jesus and the Greek wor from Canaan (a foreigner) seeking help. Jesus gives to her what see like three shocks: First, Jesus looks at her then away; second, Jesus t her that she does not belong (*mbanu, I soghi*); third. Jesus compares to a dog (*ilechaa m, m di gi ka onye gewere nri unu m tupuru nk* This woman understanding the barrier she has to overcome, is hun enough, clever enough, patient enough, resilient enough to turn Je rebuffs into an advantage.

Excuse me friend: did I hear Jesus call this needy woman a dog? N however, that Jesus is rather aiming at leading this woman and all i rejecting the prevailing Judaic mentality and to accept what Isaiah prophesied 500 years before Christ that God's promises and blessi are for all.

In the Gospel of today, therefore, the miracle is as important the correction of un-Christian mentalities, and the focus on pati persevering, persistent prayer and God's boundless love for us all. C wants all nations, all peoples, all persons to know him and love him; God desires to share his love with all of us.

Friend, just like the people of Isaiah's and Jesus' time, we may dealing in one way or the other with the reality and difficulty of accept or being accepted by others who may be different from us.

Let us pray to the God who is our common father (Abba) for the ce to have a universal horizon of perspective in our relationship h others, in our understanding of the world in which we live, in our gment over issues, and in our prayers to, and worship of God. Amen!

103.   Ezk 33:7-9; Romans 13:8-10; Matt 18:15-20

IT IS SUMMARIZED IN ONE WORD- LOVE

Friend, after hearing God's stern warning to Ezekiel: "If you do speak out to dissuade the wicked from his way, the wicked shall die his guilt, but I will hold you responsible for his death", I said "Lord h mercy on me" because I know I have some explanation to make to C for the times I did not speak out as I ought to, for the times I held b from saying what I should have said and the way I should have sai simply because I didn't want to drive people away from the Churcl appear holier-than-thou. Twenty-five years and three months ago wh was just ordained, then a young priest, I thought I was going to con the whole world. Twenty-four years later, I've found out that convert just one person is a difficult challenge.

The three Scripture texts remind us again of Christian love. Fr Ezekiel 33, we learn that it is love that must motivate you and I to ge correct one another while at the same time avoiding negativity tha often prone to seeing only the faults in others and ignoring the good of them. From St. Paul, we also learn that it is love that must cause and I to not contemplate evil thoughts or carry out evil deeds aga others. And from the Gospel, we learn that it is love that must moti you and I to go the extra mile in trying to settle our differences reconcile both at individual-personal levels and at community levels

It is true that most people do not like to change if they are comfort with their old ways of life. But we should not be discouraged in lead persons away from doing something that is harming them: be it y children, parents, friends, neighbors, etc. But always add some pra for whomever you think needs help.

The epistle of St. James 5:20 says: "Whoever brings back a sin from the error of his ways will save his [or her] soul from death and cover a multitude of sins". Amen!

4. Isaiah 55:6-9; Phil 1:20c-24, 27a; Matt 20:1-16a

GOD'S UNBELIEVABLE GENEROSITY

Friend, the parables of Jesus are designed to shock us into thinking.

We all who are employed do hope for a fair living wage from our ployers. The question is: How much will you be paid, and what will 1 consider fair enough?

The shock is how the landowner could have given the same wage to se who worked a few hours and those who labored the whole day. at would be unfair and the height of insensitivity from our human soning. This reasoning is expected because it is in our human nature feel that others got more than they deserved, and I deserved more n I got.

In the time of Jesus, people work for the day's food, and are paid he end of the day. The day's pay is just enough to provide the day's d for the family. You now understand where Jesus is coming from in ? Lord's Prayer: "Give us this day our daily bread". However, Jesus is giving a lesson on being fair, or on good management, or on labor ations. It is simply a kingdom of Heaven parable that demonstrates d's unbelievable generosity. This Parable in the Gospel according to tthew captures the mentality of Jewish Christians who have difficulty epting "pagan" Christians who came lately into the vineyard by bracing Christianity. This is to help them accept others as equals in household of God.

Today we may not have this problem, I think, as we are always happy see and welcome people back to the Church who are returning or are v converts. However, let us note from the parable that envy makes ? miserable. Let us note that we need always to focus on the positive l on our blessings and give thanks. Let us know that God's ways are our ways. Let us know that the key to joy in life is gratitude. And Eucharist (*eucharistien*) we celebrate (Holy Mass), a word meaning anksgiving", the perfect way to show God this gratitude. Amen!

105. Isaiah 5:1-7; Philippians 4:6-9; Matthew 21:33-43

Goodness and gratitude versus Wickedness and Ingratitude

Friend, I often observe how we Christians listen to the Word of (with rapt attention. This is an indication, I think, that we love the W of God. But God's Word is often sweet in the mouth and sour in stomach (Cf. Ezekiel 3:3; Revelation 10:10) because we love to hea but then it challenges our way of life.

In the song of Isaiah chapter 5, God laments: "I planted a v Instead of good grapes, it yielded me wild grapes (*Akoro M ji n M; gaa ka M gwuru ji, ihe M huru bu ede ndi muo*). God threaten demolish the vine and hand it over to wild beasts and scavengers. ' threat was fulfilled in the destruction of the temple in Jerusalem and exilic deportation of Israel into Babylon and Assyria. And in the Go according to Apostle Matthew chapter 21, Jesus tells the parable of Rich Vineyard and the Wicked Tenants.

There is a clear message we get from the above texts of Isaiah Matthew: That great care has been taken in planning a project or a p or a relationship, that all the necessary logistics have been put in p and that all the needed resources and personnel have been deploye ensure success is no guarantee that things will work out well. Yes, not enough to be positive minded; we must be positive with God commending our lives, plans and affairs to God in prayer.

Friend, the song of Isaiah and the Parable of Matthew are not (the story of God and the people of old Israel; it could, indeed, be story of God and the new Israel (the Church) and ultimately the s of God and each one of us: That often, where God had expected fr of goodness and gratitude, he had received instead wickedness ingratitude. Jesus says to us: "I am the vine, you are the branches who abides in Me and I in him, he bears much fruit, for apart from you can do nothing. If anyone does not abide in Me, he is thrown a as a branch and dries up; and they gather them, and cast them into fire and they are burned..." (John 15:5-6). We have been cultiva through the working of the Holy Spirit to yield good fruits. As Apo Paul affirms in the text from Philippians chapter 4, God expects tha nches of the vine we be true (in all circumstances to who we are as ristians), honorable (in our dealings with others), just (no matter the t) and pure in heart (for blessed are the pure in heart for they shall see d). In this way, we can bring beauty and grace into our world.

Friend, pray that God's Spirit and grace will strengthen us to avoid in lives the fruits of the wild grape from the wild vine (sexual immorality, purity and debauchery, idolatry, witchcraft hatred, discord, jealousy, of rage, selfish ambition, dissensions, factions, envy, drunkenness, ies) and to embrace always the fruits of the good grape from the good e (love, joy, peace, forbearance, kindness, goodness, faithfulness, tleness and self-control.) – Cf. Gal 5:19-23. Amen!

106.   Ezekiel 2:2-5; 2Cor 12:7-10; Mark 6:1-6

Human Weakness & Strength: What Faith Brings the Equation

In the Scripture text of Corinthians chapter 12, Apostle Paul lame that a thorn in the flesh has been given to him…and three times he begged the Lord to remove the thorn that it might leave him…but Lord replies that grace is sufficient for Paul as power is made perfec weakness.

Friend, there are speculations on what this thorn in the flesh of P could be. Could it be Paul's Ulcers or his epilepsy? Whatever that is, P knows; and God knows too. But this reminds you and me of our hun condition: No matter how pretty, how beautiful, how handsome one r look from the outside, one carries something inside (in one's stoma that stenches or smells. And no matter how accomplished one might there might still be an area in one's life that seeks for answers.

Friend, this brings us to the issue of Faith in the Gospel according St. Mark Chapter 6. In this Gospel periscope, the people of Nazareth not impressed at Jesus' lowly profile, an attitude that leads to their l of faith. Yet, this Jesus of Nazareth has become the center of civilizati dividing history into two parts: BC and AD. The very circumstance Jesus' humble background, however, reminds us that it is not only intellectually gifted, or the financially successful, or the politically str who can make a difference in society. Indeed, we all can contribute, matter our earthly status or background.

When faith remains open to truth, hope and love, God's po is released into us and our potentialities are unleashed. Without t pushing and touching Jesus can become futile spiritual gallantry jamboree (Cf. Mark 5:24-35). Faith is like a switch that turns God We pray that God's Holy Spirit will continue to lead us to discover extraordinary things God can accomplish in us through our ordin and weak humanity. Amen!

7.   Deut 6:2-6; Heb 7:23-28; Mark 12:28ᵇ-34

Letters of the Commandment & Spirit of the Commandment

In the text of Deuteronomy chapter 6, God gives the letters of
Commandment through Moses; and in the Gospel according
Apostle Mark chapter 12, Jesus offers us the spirit of the
mmandment of God which is love of God and love of neighbor;
d in the beatitudes of the sermon on the mount of Matthew 5:1-12,
us further makes concrete for us the spirit of the commandment.
us promises that if we live our lives according to this spirit, we
ll not be far from God's kingdom.

Friend, Jesus is teaching us that in our world of divergent and
flicting values, we need to stick to the Gospel values that guide
as we navigate through life. This disposition is very important
ause when it comes to salvation and eternal life, despair and
hdrawal are Satan's greatest weapons and the surest path to hell.
must be focused and determined in the journey of faith, and
ther sell-out nor give-in to anti-God forces. Even in our human
perfections, we must continue to allow God walk with us for
oever is deformed can be re-formed.

As Christians, we are expected to move beyond our natural
itations to the supernatural level; what happens inside of us
to tally with what we profess from the outside. It is true that
ough the Sacraments of Christian initiation, we are initiated
o Christianity; but the convictions we hold in the inside and the
iliations we enjoy must conform to the Faith that we profess. In
s consistency, our true freedom in Christ becomes meaningful;
erwise, we are still submitting to the yoke of slavery (CF.
latians 5:1; Luke 11:37-40).

Friend, as people of God on pilgrimage, living the spirit of God's
mmandment involves three interconnected steps: to walk, to build
d to confess. When we are no longer walking the walk of faith, we
p and are stagnant. When we are no longer building the Kingdom
God, nothing is happening. When we are no longer confessing

Christ, then we are, perhaps, confessing the devil. Friend, I inv
you: Let us do the walking together; let us do the building of
Church of Christ together; and let us confess Christ together as
family. And for these to happen (walking, building, confessin
each of us, members of Christ's church, must be ready to carry
cross daily to follow Jesus. We pray that we may continue to rece
the moral strength and spiritual courage to do exactly this. Ame

8. Gen 28:16-22; Gen 35:1-6; Gen12:7-9; Gen 13:14-18; alm

128:1-6; 2Cor 11:23b-28; Luke 18:29-31

Landmarks and Milestones!

Jacob (renamed Israel) erects a stone after a spiritual encounter :h God. This is what is called a landmark; and he comes back there er many years to worship and celebrate a successful milestone in life.

Again, Abraham erects three principal Altars (at Shechem, Bethel 1 Hebron), and traces his steps/encounters with God through the ars he builds. These are called Landmarks.

Apostle Paul recounts certain negative circumstances in his life indmarks), and despite these transitory odds, celebrates in his irt a hugely successful Evangelization by God's grace (Milestone).

Friend, along the journey of life, and in the midst of the good, bad and the ugly, God assures us of his promises and blessings f. Psalm 128:1-6; Luke 18:29-31).

Our human existence consists of Landmarks and Milestones. wever, these two words are often confused by many. Landmarks present significant historical event (positive or negative along the ·t of life's journey with God. Milestones represent celebrations (of inksgiving to God) of a chain of landmarks (significant historical :nts). These celebrations become a recall and recognition of cord Milestones emerging from historical Landmarks.

Examples of Landmarks (events) could be Births, Marriages, dinations, Graduations, Deaths, etc.

Examples of Milestones could be birthdays, anniversaries, ·ilees, graduation parties, etc.

Friend, allow me to go personal and illustrate the two terms with ermon I gave at my 50th Birthday Anniversary in 2011:

"Golden Jubilee (whether of Birth or Marriage or Ordination
Religious Profession) is one of those Milestone celebrations wl
we recall and share with others some Landmark events in our
stories. I was born premature on February 16, 1961 into the ha
of deeply Catholic Parents: late Ezinne Christiana Iheakar
Okwuchukwu Osunkwo and Ezinna Sylvester Mputam Osunk
Because I was born premature, my father who was at that ti
serving a white Missionary priest from Ireland, prayed to Apo
St. Jude Thaddeus (Patron of difficult and hopeless cases) promis
that if I survived through the intercession of St. Jude Thaddeu
would be given the name Jude Thaddeus at Baptism. He, furtl
went on to make a solemn vow to God (without consulting
anyway) that if I survived (and it pleased God to take me), he wo
dedicate me entirely to God's service. My other seven siblings i
I grew up under very strict Christian rules. Growing under a (
who was a white man's teacher and Station catechist was fun.
father served seven expatriate priests. People in those days admi
the children of the white man's teachers and treated it as a spe
privilege to visit their homes with firewood and play and inte
with their children. Of course these teachers were very few then.

Throughout the period of the Nigerian-Biafran Civil War wh
occurred between 1967 and 1970, I did my primary education w
other pupils under a war situation and environment. We had
study under bushes because of fear of the enemy (Nigerian) figl
and bomber planes. In these war years, my hometown Parish
Anthony's Parish, Isiekenesi in Orlu North-East) had a white n
from Ireland as Parish Priest, His name is Fr. McCaffrey, CSSP.
loved me so much not only because of my Dad but also beca
of the circumstances of my birth. He would always take me to
thatched residence in the Mission compound during break time
give me the white man's tea and coffee.

The war years did not affect my siblings and I adversely beca
my Father was in charge of Caritas in our area. It was my childh(
relationship with Fr. McCaffrey which ignited my desire to becon
priest. He left in 1970 after the civil war that ended with a declarat
of "No victor, No vanquished!" Because of the inner urge develop
in me at the time to become a priest, I finished my primary educat
in 1973 and had to break from formal education to do some me

s in a block molding company (named Asu Services and Supply mpany) in order to raise some money which would enable me e an entrance examination to the junior seminary. The money I ed weekly for a year enabled me to realize my dream to enter the ninary. By 1974, I had saved enough money to take the entrance mination into the Holy Ghost Juniorate Ihiala in Anambra State Nigeria, attend the interview at Ihiala with no person guiding , passed the interview and paid the advance fee, received my spectus and started seminary education by September, 1974.

Through the years of education and graduate studies spanning m 1974 to 2012 (Holy Ghost Juniorate Ihiala, Bigard Memorial jor Seminary Ikot Ekpene, Bigard Memorial Major Seminary ugu, Pontifical Urban University Rome and Graduate Theological ndation Indiana Affiliate of Oxford University of London) God ssomed me academically. In my Class of 1979 I got the best nool Certificate result with distinction and an offer of University mission into Imo State University (Aba Campus) to do Law. cause this offer was attractive to any young man then, I came a crossroad in my vocation. It was a crisis moment in my life ich confronted me with a fundamental option between becoming riest and becoming a Lawyer: I turned down the offer to do Law favor of the Priesthood, a decision which made me look stupid the eyes of my peers. In my torturous academic journey, God blessed me with the PhD honors in Theology specializing in vironmental Theology (First Class Division), the M.A. honors Missiology (First Class Division), the B.A. honors in Philosophy cond Class Upper Division). But I am not yet academically tired.

To the Glory of God, I have authored three books and one oklet: *God and the Human Environment* (2015); *Reflections for ily living* (2015); *Handbook Manual on Marriage Preparation and nily Apostolate* (2015) and *Simple Catechism Book for Youth and ing Adults* (2015)

In the area of Pastoral experience, I have had vast pastoral eriences. I have served in seven Parishes in the Orlu Catholic ocese of Nigeria: St. Gregory Parish Amaigbo; St. John Parish ualla; St. Theresa Parish Mbato; St. Paul Parish Amiri; St. ıl Parish Isu; All Saints Parish Ebenator and St. James Parish

Arondizuogu. I have also served the Diocese of Orlu as Dioce
Director of Religious Education and Diocesan Chaplain of O
Diocesan Catechists Association for four years respectively. I
a member of the National Association of Directors of Religi
Education (NADRE) Nigeria for four years. Presently, I am a F
Donum Priest to the Catholic Archdiocese of Boston, MA, US,
am currently the Parochial Vicar of the St. Katharine Drexel Par
Boston, and the Chaplain of Nigerian Catholics in the Archdioc
of Boston. I am a fourth degree member of the Knighthood
Columbus International and Chaplain to Council 15292, USA.

In all these years of Pastoral ministry, I left behind no scanda
any form. In all these places of Pastoral assignment, good memo:
have continued to follow my footprints.

Friend, you may already be thinking: Did Fr. Osunkwo e
encounter any problem along the way all these years? Your gues
as good as mine. Life is not always a bed of roses, and even if so, rc
have thorns. Life can sometimes assume an appearance of "a sug
coated bitterness". I did encounter problems: While in the Jur
Seminary at Ihiala, I was suspended indefinitely (the equivalen
expulsion in the history of the Seminary) for almost a whole sch
term for insulting a senior prefect, and was miraculously recal
after three months. I had another crisis of vocation while at Big
Memorial Major Seminary Ikot Ekpene and I had to decide to ca
a day with the priesthood and packed home. But after interventic
human and divine, I packed back to the Seminary after four mont
I have had health challenges: At one point while in Bigard Memo
Major Seminary, I became sickly, though doctors could not diagn
anything. It was my spiritual director, Rev. Fr. Anthony Njoku, v
eventually made a special prayer for me that brought me miracul
healing. I was again very ill to the point of death with an ulcer wh
bled in my stomach while studying in Rome. It was miraculous t
I was declared healed from the ulcer by two of my Doctors:
Pedona of Italy in 2009 and Dr. Resil Claude of Boston in 201
have had three ghastly car accidents (one of brake failure, one of
pull and one of another car crashing into mine). I have been attac
five times in the Parish Rectory by armed robbers. But in all th
accident and robbery attacks, not one drop of my blood was lost

Friend, looking back to these 50 years of my earthly sojourn (now 54 years), I can identify some landmarks (historical events): Circumstances of my birth, civil war primary education, circumstances of my Seminary formation, long period of educational pursuits, vast pastoral experience that cuts across the continents of Africa, Europe and America, and challenges along the way. In all these, I wish to state in truth that by God's grace and mercy, my life has been a glory to God; my life has been a divine instrument in the hands of the Church; my life has been an inestimable blessing to humanity; and my life has been an invaluable asset to my family. I thank God for all these today as I celebrate with family and friends milestones of accomplishments that cut across the personal, the filial, the pastoral, the missionary and the academic. In the name of God, I thank and bless all those who have stood by me. May your genuine dreams come true. Amen!

Inspirational Meditation Songs/Lyrics

God Of Mercy And Compassion (unknown author)

1. God of mercy and compassion,
Look with pity upon me,
Father, let me call Thee Father,
'Tis Thy child returns to Thee.

Refrain:
Jesus, Lord, I ask for mercy;
Let me not implore in vain;
All my sins, I now detest them,
Never will I sin again.

2. By my sins I have deserved
Death and endless misery,
Hell with all its pains and torments,
And for all eternity.
(Refrain)

3. By my sins I have abandoned
Right and claim to heav'n above.
Where the saints rejoice forever
In a boundless sea of love.
(Refrain)

4. See our Savior, bleeding, dying,
On the cross of Calvary;
To that cross my sins have nail'd Him,
Yet He bleeds and dies for me.
(Refrain)

Gregorian Chant Lyrics

My soul is longing for your peace (Lucien Deiss)

Refrain:

My soul is longing for your peace,
near to you, my God!

Lord, you know that my heart is not proud,
And my eyes are not lifted from the earth.

Lofty thoughts have never filled my mind,
Far beyond my sight all ambitious deeds.

In your peace I have maintained my soul,
I have kept my heart in your quiet peace.
As a child rests on his mother's knee
So I place my soul in your loving care

Israel, put all your hope in God.
Give the Lord your trust, now and evermore.

How Great Thou Art (Stuart K. Hine)

O Lord my God when I in awesome wonder.

Consider all the world your hands have made.

I see the stars, I hear the rolling thunder.

Thy power throughout the universe displayed.

Then sings my soul, my savior God to me.

How great though art, How great though art.

Then sings my soul, my savior God to me.

How great though art, How great though art.

And when I think that God his son not sparing.

Sent him to die, I scarce can take it in.

That on the cross, my burden gladly bearing.

He bled and died to take away my sins.

Then sings my soul, my savior God to me.

How great though art, How great though art.

Then sings my soul, my savior God to me.

How great though art, How great though art.

Amazing Grace (John Newton)

Amazing Grace, how sweet the sound,

That saved a wretch like me.

I once was lost but now am found,

Was blind, but now I see.

T'was Grace that taught my heart to fear.

And Grace, my fears relieved.

How precious did that Grace appear,

The hour I first believed.

Through many dangers, toils and snares,

I have already come;

'Twas Grace, that brought me safe thus far,

and Grace will lead me home.

The Lord has promised good to me.

His word my hope secures.

He will my shield and portion be,

As long as life endures.

When we've been here ten thousand years,

Bright shining, as the sun.

We've no less days to sing God's praise

Than when we've first begun.

All the Earth Proclaim the Lord (Lucien Deiss)

Refrain:

All the earth proclaim the Lord,

Sing your praise to God.

1. Serve you the Lord, heart filled with gladness.

Come into His Presence singing for joy.

2. Know that the Lord is our creator.

Yes, he is our Father; we are His own.

3. We are the sheep of His green pasture.

For we are His people; He is our God.

4. Enter His gates bringing thanksgiving,

O enter His courts while singing His praise.

5. Our Lord is good, His love enduring,

His word is abiding now with us all.

6. Honor and praise be to the Father.

The Son, and the Spirit, world without end.

I Surrender (Judson W. Van DeVenter)

1   All to Jesus I surrender;
All to Him I freely give;
I will ever love and trust Him,
In His presence daily live.

Refrain:

I surrender all,

I surrender all;

All to Thee, my blessed Savior,

I surrender all.

2   All to Jesus I surrender;

Humbly at His feet I bow,

Worldly pleasures all forsaken;

Take me, Jesus, take me now.

3   All to Jesus I surrender;

Make me, Savior, wholly thine;

Let me feel the Holy Spirit,

Truly know that Thou art mine.

4   All to Jesus I surrender;

Lord, I give myself to Thee;

Fill me with Thy love and power;

Let Thy blessing fall on me.

5   All to Jesus I surrender;

Now I feel the sacred flame.

Oh, the joy of full salvation!

Glory, glory, to His Name!

Keep in Mind (Lucien Deiss)

Refrain:

Keep in mind that Jesus Christ has died for us
and is risen from the dead.
He is our saving Lord;
he is joy for all ages.

1   If we die with the Lord, we shall live with the Lord.
If we endure with the Lord, we shall live with the Lord. (Refrain)

2   In him all our sorrow, in him all our joy.
In him hope of glory, in him all our love. (Refrain)

3   In him our redemption, in him all our grace.
In him our salvation, in him all our peace. (Refrain)

Blessed Assurance (Phoebe Knapp)

1   Blessed assurance, Jesus is mine!
Oh, what a foretaste of glory divine!
Heir of salvation, purchase of God,
Born of His Spirit, washed in His blood.

Refrain:

This is my story, this is my song,

Praising my Savior all the day long;

This is my story, this is my song,

Praising my Savior all the day long.

2   Perfect submission, perfect delight,

Visions of rapture now burst on my sight;

Angels, descending, bring from above

Echoes of mercy, whispers of love.

3   Perfect submission, all is at rest,

I in my Savior am happy and blest,

Watching and waiting, looking above,

Filled with His goodness, lost in His love

It's Not An Easy Road (John Barnett)_

1. It's not an easy road we are trav'ling to Heaven,

For many are the thorns on the way;

It's not an easy road but the Savior is with us,

His presence gives us joy ev'ry day.

Refrain:

No, no, it's not an easy road,

No, no, it's not an easy road.

But Jesus walks with me and brightens my journey,

And lightens ev'ry heavy load.

2. It's not an easy road, there are trials and troubles,

And many are the dangers we meet;

But Jesus guards and keeps so that nothing can harm us,

And smooth the rugged path for our feet.

3. Tho' I am often footsore and weary from travel,

Tho' I am often bowed down with care;

 A better day is coming when Home in the glory,

We'll rest in perfect peace over there.

Yes I shall arise and return to my Father! (Lucien Dei⟨

Refrain:

Yes I shall arise and return to my Father!

1. To you, O Lord, I lift up my soul;
In you, O my God, I place all my trust.

2. Look down on me, have mercy, O Lord;
Forgive me my sins, behold all my grief.

3. My heart and soul shall yearn for your face;
Be gracious to me and answer my plea.

4. Do not withhold your goodness from me;
O Lord, may your love be deep in my soul;

5. To you I pray; have pity on me;
My God, I have sinned against your great love.

6. Mercy, I cry, O Lord, wash me clean;
And wither than snow my spirit shall be.

7. Give me again the joy of your help;
Now open my lips, your praise I will sing.

8. Happy is he, forgiven by God;
His sins blotted out, his guilt is no more

O Lord I am Not Worthy (Gregorian)

1. O Lord, I am not worthy
That Thou should'st come to me,
But speak the words of comfort,
My spirit healed shall be.

2. Oh, come, all you who labor
In sorrow and in pain,
Come, eat This Bread from heaven;
Thy peace and strength regain.

3. O Jesus, we adore Thee,
Our Victim and our Priest,
Whose precious Blood and Body
Become our sacred Feast.

4. O Sacrament most holy,
O Sacrament divine!
All praise and all thanksgiving
Be ev'ry moment Thine.

Holy God, We Praise Thy Name (Clarence Walworth)

1. Holy God, we praise Thy Name;
Lord of all, we bow before Thee!
All on earth Thy scepter claim,
All in heaven above adore Thee;
Infinite Thy vast domain,
Everlasting is Thy reign.

2. Hark! the loud celestial hymn
Angel choirs above are raising,
Cherubim and seraphim,
In unceasing chorus praising;
Fill the heavens with sweet accord:
Holy, holy, holy, Lord.
3. Lo! the apostolic train
Join the sacred Name to hallow;
Prophets swell the loud refrain,
And the white-robed martyrs follow;
And from morn to set of sun,
Through the Church the song goes on.

4. Holy Father, Holy Son,
Holy Spirit, Three we name Thee;
While in essence only One,
Undivided God we claim Thee;
And adoring bend the knee,
While we own the mystery.

Pass Me Not, O Gentle Savoir (William H. Doane)

1. Pass me not, O gentle Savior,
Hear my humble cry;
While on others Thou art calling,
Do not pass me by.

Refrain
Savior, Savior,
Hear my humble cry;
While on others Thou art calling
Do not pass me by.

2. Let me at Thy throne of mercy
Find a sweet relief,
Kneeling there in deep contrition;
Help my unbelief.

3. Trusting only in Thy merit,
Would I seek Thy face;
Heal my wounded, broken spirit,
Save me by Thy grace.

4. Thou the Spring of all my comfort,
More than life to me,
Whom have I on earth beside Thee?
Whom in heav'n but Thee?

It Is Well With My Soul (Philip Bliss)

1. When peace like a river, attendeth my way,
When sorrows like sea billows roll;
Whatever my lot, Thou hast taught me to *know*,
It is well, it is well, with my soul.

Refrain:
It is well, (it is well),
With my soul, (with my soul)
It is well, it is well, with my soul.

2. Though Satan should buffet, though trials should come,
Let this blest assurance control,
That Christ has regarded my helpless estate,
And hath shed His own blood for my soul.

3. My sin, oh, the bliss of this glorious thought!
My sin, not in part but the whole,
Is nailed to the cross, and I bear it no more,
Praise the Lord, praise the Lord, O my soul!

4. For me, be it Christ, be it Christ hence to live:
If Jordan above me shall roll,
No pang shall be mine, for in death as in life,
Thou wilt whisper Thy peace to my soul.

5. But Lord, 'tis for Thee, for Thy coming we wait,

The sky, not the grave, is our goal;

Oh, trump of the angel! Oh, voice of the Lord!

Blessed hope, blessed rest of my soul.

6. And Lord, haste the day when my faith shall be sight,

The clouds be rolled back as a scroll;

The trump shall resound, and the Lord shall descend,

Even so, it is well with my soul.

Salve Regina (Hermann of Reichenau)

47   48   49

Salve Regina,

Mater Misericordiae

Vita dulcedo

et spes nostra salve

Ad te clamamus,

exsules filii Hevae

Ad te suspiramus,

gementes et flentes

In hac lacrimarum valle

Eia, ergo, advocata nostra

illos tuos misericordes oculos ad nos converte

Et Iesum, benedictum fructum ventris tui

Nobis post hoc exsilium ostende

O clemens, O pia, O dulcis, Virgo Maria

50   51

Hail Queen of Heaven, the Ocean Star (John Lingard)

Hail, Queen of heaven, the ocean star,
Guide of the wanderer here below,
Thrown on life's surge, we claim thy care,
Save us from peril and from woe.

Mother of Christ, Star of the sea
Pray for the wanderer, pray for me.

O gentle, chaste, and spotless Maid,
We sinners make our prayers through thee;
Remind thy Son that He has paid
The price of our iniquity.

Virgin most pure, Star of the sea,
Pray for the sinner, pray for me.

Sojourners in this vale of tears,
Blest advocate, to thee we cry,
Assuage our sorrows, calm our fears,
And soothe with hope our misery.

Refuge in grief, Star of the sea
Pray for the mourner, pray for me.

And while to Him Who reigns above
In Godhead one, in Persons three,
The Source of life, of grace, of love,
Homage we pay on bended knee:

Do thou, bright Queen, Star of the sea,
Pray for thy children, pray for me.

Abide with Me (Henry Francis Lyte)

Abide with me; fast falls the eventide;

The darkness deepens; Lord with me abide.

When other helpers fail and comforts flee,

Help of the helpless, O abide with me.

Swift to its close ebbs out life's little day;

Earth's joys grow dim; its glories pass away;

Change and decay in all around I see;

O Thou who changest not, abide with me.

Not a brief glance I beg, a passing word,

But as Thou dwell'st with Thy disciples, Lord,

Familiar, condescending, patient, free.

Come not to sojourn, but abide with me.

Come not in terrors, as the King of kings,

But kind and good, with healing in Thy wings;

Tears for all woes, a heart for every plea.

Come, Friend of sinners, thus abide with me.

Thou on my head in early youth didst smile,

And though rebellious and perverse meanwhile,

Thou hast not left me, oft as I left Thee.

On to the close, O Lord, abide with me.

I need Thy presence every passing hour.

What but Thy grace can foil the tempter's power?

Who, like Thyself, my guide and stay can be?

Through cloud and sunshine, Lord, abide with me.

I fear no foe, with Thee at hand to bless;

Ills have no weight, and tears no bitterness.

Where is death's sting? Where, grave, thy victory?

I triumph still, if Thou abide with me.

Hold Thou Thy cross before my closing eyes;

Shine through the gloom and point me to the skies.

Heaven's morning breaks, and earth's vain shadows flee;

In life, in death, O Lord, abide with me.

<u>Praise to the Holiest in the height</u> (John Henry Newm.

Praise to the Holiest in the height,

and in the depth be praise;

in all his words most wonderful,

most sure in all his ways!

O loving wisdom of our God!

When all was sin and shame,

a second Adam to the fight

and to the rescue came.

O wisest love! that flesh and blood,

which did in Adam fail,

should strive afresh against the foe,

should strive, and should prevail;

and that the highest gift of grace

should flesh and blood refine:

God's presence and his very self,

and essence all-divine.

O generous love! that he who smote

in man for ma the foe,

the double agony in Man

for man should undergo.

And in the garden secretly,
and on the cross on high,
should teach his brethren, and inspire
to suffer and to die.

Praise to the Holiest in the height,
and in the depth be praise;
in all his words most wonderful,
most sure in all his ways!

Come Holy Ghost Creator Come (Thomas Tallis)

Come, Holy Ghost, Creator, come

From Thy bright heav'nly throne;

Come, take possession of our souls,

And make them all Thine own.

Thou who art called the Paraclete,

Best gift of God above,

The living spring, the living fire,

Sweet unction and true love.

Thou who art sevenfold in Thy grace,

Finger of God's right hand;

His promise, teaching little ones

To speak and understand.

O guide our minds with Thy blest light,

With love our hearts inflame;

And with Thy strength, which ne'er decays,

Confirm our mortal frame.

Far from us drive our deadly foe;

True peace unto us bring;

And through all perils lead us safe

Beneath Thy sacred wing.

Through Thee may we the Father know,

Through Thee th'eternal Son,

And Thee the Spirit of them both,

Thrice-blessèd Three in One.

All glory to the Father be,

With His co-equal Son:

The same to Thee, great Paraclete,

While endless ages run.

Now it is Evening (P. Herbert)

Now it is evening; time to cease from labor,
Father, according to thy will and pleasure,
Through the night-season, have thy faithful people
Safe in thy keeping.

Far from our dwellings drive the evil spirits;
Under the shadow of thy wings protect us;
Be thou our guardian through the hours of darkness,
Strong to defend us.

Call we, ere sleeping, on the name of Jesus;
Rise we at day-break, strong to serve thee better;
Order our goings, well begun and ended,
All to thy glory.

Fountain of goodness, bless the sick and needy;
Visit the captive, solace the afflicted;
Shelter the stranger, feed your starving children;
Strengthen the dying.

Father, who neither slumberest nor sleepest,
Thou, to whom darkness is as clear as noonday,
Safe in thy keeping.

Lead, Kindly Light (John Henry Newman)

Lead, kindly Light, amid th' encircling gloom, lead Thou me on!

The night is dark, and I am far from home; lead Thou me on!

Keep Thou my feet; I do not ask to see

The distant scene; one step enough for me.

I was not ever thus, nor prayed that Thou shouldst lead me on;

I loved to choose and see my path; but now lead Thou me on!

I loved the garish day, and, spite of fears,

Pride ruled my will. Remember not past years!

So long Thy power hath blest me, sure it still will lead me on.

O'er moor and fen, o'er crag and torrent, till the night is gone,

And with the morn those angel faces smile, which I

Have loved long since, and lost awhile!

Meantime, along the narrow rugged path, Thyself hast trod,

Lead, Savior, lead me home in childlike faith, home to my God.

To rest forever after earthly strife

In the calm light of everlasting life.

Lord of all hopefulness (Jan Struther)

Lord of all hopefulness, Lord of all joy,

Whose trust, ever childlike, no cares can destroy,

Be there at our waking, and give us, we pray,

Your bliss in our hearts, Lord, at the break of the day.

Lord of all eagerness, Lord of all faith,

Whose strong hands were skilled at the plane and the lathe,

Be there at our labors, and give us, we pray,

Your strength in our hearts, Lord at the noon of the day.

Lord of all kindliness, Lord of all grace,

Your hands swift to welcome, your arms to embrace,

Be there at our homing, and give us, we pray,

Your love in our hearts, Lord, at the eve of the day.

Lord of all gentleness, Lord of all calm,

Whose voice is contentment, whose presence is balm,

Be there at our sleeping, and give us, we pray,

Your peace in our hearts, Lord, at the end of the day.

Trust and Obey (John H. Sammis)

When we walk with the Lord in the light of His Word,
What a glory He sheds on our way!
While we do His good will, He abides with us still,
And with all who will trust and obey.

Refrain:

Trust and obey, for there's no other way

To be happy in Jesus, but to trust and obey.

Not a shadow can rise, not a cloud in the skies,

But His smile quickly drives it away;

Not a doubt or a fear, not a sigh or a tear,

Can abide while we trust and obey.

Not a burden we bear, not a sorrow we share,

But our toil He doth richly repay;

Not a grief or a loss, not a frown or a cross,

But is blessed if we trust and obey.

But we never can prove the delights of His love

Until all on the altar we lay;

For the favor He shows, for the joy He bestows,

Are for them who will trust and obey.

Then in fellowship sweet we will sit at His feet,

Or we'll walk by His side in the way;

What He says we will do, where He sends we will go;

Never fear, only trust and obey.

OTHER HYMNS

I bu Chineke, I bughi Mmadu

Atukwasara M gi obi Chineke (Ekwela k'ihere mee M o Chine
Ekela uwa kuo M onu

Aga m ebuli aha Gi elu

Yes my Lord is Able (For he has come to redeem us, he sets
captives free, he's awesome God, working on the waters of the Sea)

Bulie Ya elu

Ejiri M gi mere Nna

Obara n'eme mma/n;agwo oria/n'asa njo

Anyi n'asu Gi dalu

CPSIA information can be obtained at www.ICGtesting.com
Printed in the USA
BVOW06s0624080915

416172BV00002B/4/P